ESSAYS ON LITERARY CRITICISM
AND THE ENGLISH TRADITION

ESSAYS ON

Literary Criticism

AND THE ENGLISH TRADITION

S. L. Bethell

London

DENNIS DOBSON LTD

*First published in Great Britain in
1948 by Dennis Dobson Ltd,
12 Park Place, St James,
London SW1*

PRINTED IN GREAT BRITAIN BY
LETCHWORTH PRINTERS LTD., LETCHWORTH, HERTS
72.R

Contents

5

For
GILBERT SHAW
friend and counsellor;
as a humble contribution
towards the desired
synthesis

Prefatory Note

THESE ESSAYS FIRST APPEARED in the *New English Weekly*, during the Winter and Spring of 1945-6. My thanks are due to the Editor for permission to publish them in this form. In revising them I have restored certain passages which the exigencies of periodical publication in an acute paper shortage had compelled me to omit, and I have made some corrections and additions. The alterations have not, however, been extensive. I have not attempted to remove the time-references which indicate the periodic and occasional composition of these essays; to have done so might have suggested that I put them forward as a formal treatise, whereas in fact they are concerned only with certain problems which seem to be especially important at the present time. I cannot trace my various indebtedness for proper acknowledgement but, as Dr Leavis and the periodical *Scrutiny* receive a good deal of attention and some adverse criticism in the following pages, it is right to point out that I have read all the writings of Dr Leavis and every issue of *Scrutiny* since its inception, always with great profit though with frequent disagreement. *Scrutiny* kept criticism alive in the worst days, and we are grateful. As for Dr Leavis, the influence of his thought and critical practice

7

upon my own has been so great that, in working towards what I hope is a more comprehensive position, the best way that I can argue with myself is by arguing with him. It is only in this sense that my criticism is to be regarded as 'personal'.

S.L.B.

I *Of Criticism*

THE LITERARY CRITIC SPENDS much of his time in apologizing for his own existence. He is generally believed to be a charlatan and people tell him with disarming frankness that that is what he is: 'Oh, but surely it's all a matter of taste?' His reply, 'Yes, madam, *good* taste and *bad* taste', is frequently resented. No other profession suffers in quite the same way. Imagine it: 'But, doctor, I insist on having those little white pills. Any one can see they're better than this horrid brown liquid you've given me'—or 'Why do you engineers force your tastes upon the public? The bridge would be far more satisfactory if it were a perfect arc.' The unlimited assertion of private judgement is usually found in matters of secondary importance, that is, in our day, matters which do not seem to involve the safety of lives and property. So in religion tolerance has increased with the weakening of belief; when the eternal destiny of the soul was the great reality before men's minds, it did not occur to them to tolerate beliefs which made for the soul's perdition. If the tranquillity of the world were seen strangely to depend upon a proper estimate of Shakespeare's *Hamlet*, Goethe's *Faust* and Tolstoi's *War and Peace*, we can imagine the conference of critics that would be called—

9

with a passing shudder at its probable composition
—and the meek submission with which the Great
Public would attend its verdict.

But the critics of the critics are not entirely
wrong. Criticism naturally develops late, and,
except for a fair proportion of Johnson, Coleridge
and Arnold, there is not much in the literary criticism of the past to commend it to a modern reader.
Either it treated of technical questions—syllable-
counting and 'true' rhymes, the differences of epic
and dramatic—or it gossipped interestingly of
books and characters; its discipline was either
superficial or non-existent. No wonder it was
scorned as a parasite upon creative literature,
especially in the last century when so much that
passed for criticism was in reality the writer's own
meditative variations upon the theme of his original, an outlet for frustrated creation. It is in our
own time that criticism has shown itself to be important and its best days are probably yet to come.

The salient fact about contemporary culture is
that it is not truly a culture at all. It is not based
upon a commonly held system of unconscious
assumptions—dogmas, in the sense in which Dr
Demant uses the word; there is, rather, a common
belief that such unquestioned assumptions are no
longer possible in an age of psychological enlighten-
ment. And no traditional system of philosophy
seems likely to win general acceptance in the teeth
of what Professor Hodges calls 'the critique'. In
this situation what binds us together is a common
sense of inadequacy, which is not in itself a bad
thing, and a less healthy fear of imminent cultural

collapse. The natural tendency, therefore, is to search the past in order to understand what we have lost and to obtain guidance for the future, and the unprofessional philosopher, the writer on cultural problems, whose concern is the practical reason and practical certitude, seems inclined to proceed on the assumption that an adequate account of cultural history would bring us as near to universal truth as we are likely to attain; if we can show that certain beliefs are necessary to a fully human life, it would seem likely that those beliefs approximate to the truth. Perhaps the one advantage of living in an age without a culture is that for such an age the cultures of the past become of immediate and living importance; history is gathered up in the eternal moment of our own dubious present. Here, then, is a new dignity and a new task for the literary critic, since it would, I think, be pretty generally agreed that more aspects of a culture lie open to investigation in its literature than in any other mode of expression. 'Le style, c'est l'homme même', but the man is to a great extent a product of his age, and so is his style which the critic examines. It would be untrue to say that the new psychological techniques have provided the critic with a method (Dr Richards is best when he forgets his more than doubtful psychology) but they have suggested an adjustment of his attention, from the explicit to the implicit, so that he may now draw to light and examine those fundamental 'dogmas' or assumptions of which his author was for the most part unconscious since they were so much a part of himself. An author is thus assessed upon his fundamental attitudes to life, with, of course, the adequacy of their expression; he is placed in the context of his period and the period itself evaluated in him and related to the wider movement of cultural history which records the fluctuations of the human spirit in its dealings with the eternal.

When in pursuing this sociological method I first pointed out the intimate relation between literary criticism and theology, my findings were coldly received and one lady, intelligent enough to know better, accused me of reviving the fallacies of Jeremy Collier. It was, of course, far from my intention to suggest that a work of art should be judged solely on its explicit ethical or theological teaching, and I can only believe that the lady in question read my careful and designedly elementary explanation on a drowsy Sunday afternoon. For, if criticism implies an assessment of value, how can it be divorced from theological considerations? There are some who assert that the sole function of the critic is to answer the question, 'Has the author succeeded in doing what he set out to do?' I do not know how, apart from divine inspiration, they can be certain of an author's intentions, and in any event so often in a work of art something is achieved both beyond and different from the original conscious design. And would any one be content with a critic who declined to rank Shakespeare above Mr Noel Coward on any ground except the very doubtful one of his greater success in carrying out his intentions? At least in literature 'success' is an inadequate criterion. Moreover, there is no

12

purely aesthetic standard in literary criticism, or if you prefer it, the aesthetic judgement is formed not only upon aesthetic content and adequacy of expression but upon importance of material and depth of insight as well. Prior's little drawing-room verses to Chloe and the rest are perfectly successful; they are 'better' than the complete flop of Cowley's pretentious *Davideis* but not so 'good' as the imperfect *Hamlet* or the uneven *David Copperfield*. Dr Leavis has more than once stated that literary criticism involves ethical considerations, and it is obvious that we cannot discuss a writer's 'insight' without having some standard by which to assess it. But Dr Leavis has nowhere said that theological considerations are also necessary; indeed he would seem to believe the contrary. Yet, even apart from the fact that there are insights which are spiritual without being ethical, does not the acceptance of an ethical position in itself involve at least some relation to the systems of theology? If the critic elects to take his stand on 'ethics' without any philosophical examination of the matter, there will always be a chance that his ethics may consist of personal predilections or the assumptions of his own social group. Whether this is so will be apparent to readers of *Scrutiny*.

It is often urged that there would be little practical difference between the literary judgements of Christian and non-Christian critics. For the moment this is largely true, though the Marxist opinion of Mr Eliot as the last kick of a dying *bourgeoisie* would meet with opposition from some of us and it appears that ethical and political con-

siderations founded in theology produce diverse
estimates of the value of Charlotte M. Yonge's
novels. But what of the old platitude that we are
still living on the accumulated capital of a Christian past? Does it not apply to our literary as well
as our moral judgement, and because the one is
implied in the other? The majority today prefer
'swing' to Bach and Coward to Shakespeare. No
doubt majorities have always liked the wrong
things (though less noticeably in Shakespeare's
time, to judge by his commercial success) but
whereas in the past minority opinion controlled
the effective culture, that is not quite so today and
is likely to be even less so in the future. Are we to
blame if we seek secure foundations in an age of in-
security? Criticism should be the dominant literary
activity in our time, for with us creation is an accident or rather an act of extraordinary grace. But
criticism of a destructive kind we were born to, and
it will go hard with us if we cannot divert that
energy to a constructive task, perfecting the instru-
ment and justifying our belief in it not so much by
argument, as here, but by a newly acquired insight
through literature into history and a consequent
revision of our ideas regarding the nature and
destiny of man.

II *The Critical Analogy*

THE LITERARY CRITIC NEEDS theology in his service and in turn, through the discovery of our cultural history, serves a theological end. This is a practical statement, not primarily a matter of theory, and the critic who disagrees with it is quite justified in doing so, since no doubt his own literary criticism works by a different process towards a different end. If his process be defective and his end inadequate, that will not become apparent to him until he has first perceived a number of important truths that have little immediate connection with literary criticism.

Meanwhile the Christian critic must continue in his function with little hope of general acceptance, contributing his quota to what we hope will be the Christian synthesis of the twentieth century. And if I am right in supposing that literary criticism is the dominant or characteristic activity of the contemporary intelligence, it may well provide the nucleus of that synthesis towards which we are working. The old philosophical systems have gone down before the onslaught of the philosophical critique, perhaps in order to teach us a spiritual as well as an intellectual lesson. God's universe cannot be known by the categories of logic and the methods of science; as Dr Lampert has pointed out

15

in that remarkable book *The Divine Realm,* we
cannot circumscribe the creative activity of a personal God within the clumsy framework of caus-
ality. In this respect the Aristotelian universe of St
Thomas is as much a scientific structure as the universe of Newton or Leibnitz. The literary critic,
however, reads a poem to reach the poet's mind,
not by formal logic or the regular inductive method
but by a general sensitiveness to impressions, catch-
ing a hint here and there, allowing his emotions to
be stirred and directed, not resisting if he should
become favourably inclined towards the work and
its author. His tentative approaches are those of
the would-be friend or lover and his facts are a
tissue of delicately observed imponderables. We are
accustomed to being told that the whole creation
is a poem; it is a trite and sentimental observation
which I do not think is usually taken as seriously
as it ought to be. Miss Dorothy Sayers in *The Mind
of the Maker,* which I must confess I have not read,
treats, I understand, the analogy between literary
and divine creation. What I am suggesting is a
related but not identical analogy, that between the
reader of a poem and the ordinary man in his day-
to-day experience of living. For it is only by living
that we may discern the meaning of life; it is untrue that the spectator sees most of this game, yet
the philosopher has too often been content with a
grandstand seat. We come to understand life—and
therefore Nature and God—as we come to understand a wife, by living with her, not by calculations
based upon her age and weight; and as we come
to understand a poem by its effect upon us, not

by counting the number of words in each stanza.

With the collapse of formal logic and the over-throw of strictly formal metaphysics we urgently need a new standpoint from which to attempt a reasonable understanding of the world we live in. The normal intellect cannot be satisfied with pure-ly destructive activity; agnosticism except for the philosopher *qua* philosopher is an unhealthy state of mind. 'Semantics' and recent philosophical studies of imagery, symbol and myth show the di-rection in which thought is moving. What we need for our intellectual satisfaction is a new approach to the problem of knowledge. The human mind, we are told, cannot attain to a metaphysic by the exercise of pure reason; but has any one apart from philosophers and pseudo-scientists ever suggested that purely rational processes are the only way to the truth? Has any supposedly rational, philosophi-cal system ever really satisfied men's minds? The real trouble with the systems is not that they were insufficiently logical and rational; it is rather that their logical and rational method necessarily shut off the systematizers at the very beginning of their thought-processes from much of the data which clamoured for their attention. And beginning with a parcel of thin abstractions they could hardly by thinking conjure a full-bodied universe out of it.

The failures of philosophers are in the main failures of insight, partly a result of their formal and schematic approach to experience. You cannot give an adequate account of a poem if you do not see what is really there. Your account of *Macbeth* will be defective if you have read it as just another

17

'blood and thunder'—or as exemplifying the Aristotelian tragic formula. So with the world. Yet if you strive, with Descartes, to approach experience afresh, unbiased by inherited notions, your experience will be evacuated of meaning, unless by some shift you can bring in those notions again, as Descartes did under the guise of innate ideas. This looks very like a dilemma. The philosopher needs the data of experience before he can construct a system of belief, yet he needs a system of belief in order to have any meaningful experience. Are we not virtually admitting the existence of a vicious circle of human belief, arbitrarily devised, out of which it is impossible to break into the truth? I do not think so. It is necessary to have some ideas about life in order to find any meaning in a poem or novel, and yet that poem or novel can react back upon our preconceived notions, amplifying and correcting them. Philosophies are not really made in isolation and imposed upon experience later; they are made and unmade and remade—even the most abstract of them—by the pressure of experience upon the contemplative mind. If this is so, it follows that the most fruitful method for the philosopher is not that of juggling with a few highly abstract principles but the opening of the mind to the widest and deepest range of experience—and that that philosophy will be likely to be truest which touches life at most points, not that which most completely explains away the diversity of phenomena.

This process of 'learning by experience' is the way of the literary critic and the way of the man in the street; it is also the way of the saint and the sage. I am not thinking of technically 'religious experience', mystical states or the numinous, but of the ordinary daily round in which the holy soul has acquaintance with God, knowing Him in his acts as we know our daily companions. The difficulty for the philosopher is to test and authenticate the wisdom of common life, to show us how it works and what validity it bears. Quite how he is to do so I cannot see, but perhaps the analogy of criticism may help. Meanwhile the poets would tell us that this wisdom comes of love, and love, the theologians say, is a gift of the Spirit.

III   *Mr Charles Morgan and the Nature of Criticism*   ·

ON THE TWENTY-THIRD Sunday after Trinity, being the eve of Powder Plot Day, Mr Charles Morgan read himself in as literary critic to the *Sunday Times* with a profession of faith which, at least on the surface, seems the precise converse of my own as given in the first essay of this series. It was a careful and quietly reasonable statement, so cogent as to lead astray, if it were possible, even the elect. Mr Morgan is to be admired for putting his cards on the table and the frank and decided gesture of his 'Approach to Criticism' calls for serious consideration. My own essay 'Of Criticism' was already in proof and there was no time for additions and added emphases, so I hope I may be forgiven for going over some of that ground again more thoroughly with Mr Morgan's opinions specially in mind. In one sentence we have the core of Mr Morgan's belief: 'This striving to see and to interpret works of art as they are in themselves and not in their relationship to some doctrine, religious, political, or economic, alien to their aesthetic purpose, is, as I understand it, the key to honest criticism.' He goes on: 'If I, not being of the Church of Rome, were to attack the novel or the poem of a Catholic because I did not

20

share its religious outlook, I should be guilty of stupid irrelevance', and he concludes this important paragraph by declaring that phrases such as 'Marxian criticism' or 'Modernistic criticism' are contradictions in terms. 'Christian criticism' is not mentioned but I suppose it would share Mr Morgan's strictures.

Now it seems to me that the question is begged in the first sentence quoted—and specifically in the phrase 'alien to their aesthetic purpose'; I should affirm that doctrine of many kinds is usually closely entangled with what I should prefer to call the 'aesthetic function' of a work of art. The other operative phrase in the same sentence is 'works of art as they are in themselves', which would lead us off again in the fruitless search for the *Ding an sich*. I cannot see that there is such a thing as a work of art *in itself;* a work of art is the expression of a state of mind, compounded of attitudes to 'experience' or 'life' or 'the universe', whichever term you prefer. And that inevitably brings us face to face with problems of belief and value. Let me at once clear away the most fruitful source of confusion in this matter by declaring my general agreement with the second sentence I have quoted from Mr Morgan: to attack the novel or the poem of a Catholic just because you are yourself not a Catholic is to incur guilt as a critic— and, of course, for a Catholic to attack a non-Catholic work on corresponding grounds is equally culpable. It is not quite to be guilty of 'stupid irrelevance', however; it is rather to be guilty of not having done the job thoroughly enough. The

professed doctrine of a writer is no adequate guide
to the actual content and value of his work.

The Christian critic does not automatically
approve the works of his fellow Christians. Cut-
ting across all questions of creed and class and
period there are the two broad categories of those
who can really write and those who cannot; this
is a matter of natural endowment and careful
discipline, of imagination and the proper handling
of words. If the Christian writer is no true writer
at all, then out he goes! We should like a Christian architect to build our new church, but he
must be a good architect as well as a good Christian. Even granting our Christian writer to be a
good writer, imaginative, gifted and trained in the
use of words, another question would remain. Is
his Christianity central to his experience or is it
superficial and peripheral? Is this a work of Christian insight or perhaps of some other kind of insight which may masquerade even to the writer
himself as Christian? If the former, of course as
a Christian I shall approve; if the latter I shall
need to examine still further the quality of insight
that is really there; for every glimpse of reality is
welcome to the Christian; he has inherited the
earth and those who are not against him are on
his side. It may be that our Christian writer is a
good pagan at heart—and there is a dearth of good
pagans in these days. We should welcome him. I
do not wish to labour a point which I must crave
indulgence for having raised at all; some of my
readers must be weary of my reiterated arguments
on this theme. My excuse is that I am not flogging

a dead horse; it certainly looked lively enough last Sunday and responsive to Mr Morgan's practised hand. From the Christian critic's treatment of the Christian writer, as I have tried to outline it, it should be obvious what his treatment of the non-Christian writer will be. He will not be put off by a professed Marxism or Mohammedanism or even Yoga; he will try to find out what is really there, perhaps well below the surface—and if he find anything of value he will applaud it. And, as he has to deal with the psychological complication of a possible cleavage between overt and implied beliefs, so also he has to face the complexity which arises from the fact that every writer is not only an individual but a member of a society with which he may be in or out of accord. There is the problem of the Christian in a non-Christian society and the problem of the non-Christian in a Christian society. Roughly speaking they are both with us today, for the Christian writer in contemporary England is often a product of a predominantly non-Christian environment and yet the non-Christian writer of today cannot be understood apart from the vestigial Christianity of our social order. There is a good deal of disentangling to be done in order to see what is really there, to define the quality of a modern novel or poem and assess its value for the Christian reader.

All this has taken us, I hope, a long way from the crudely dogmatic position rightly condemned by Mr Morgan. Yet I fear that my exposition of Christian criticism would fail to satisfy him. If I may be allowed the conjecture, I should imagine that he would take me back to the point at which I stated that there are two main categories of writer, the good and the bad, and ask me, 'Why not leave it at that?' This is the crucial question. Can we not be content with a criticism which merely shows which writers can and which cannot do their job satisfactorily? I do not think that we could in fact find many literary critics who would be content with so restricted and relatively uninteresting a task. For the bad writer in this sense hardly comes in for consideration at all; he is easily dismissed. Shakespeare and Mr Noel Coward, Dickens and Edgar Wallace are all good. They each have imagination of a sort and ability to achieve their ends by a skilled use of words. Deeper qualitative differences, although they may appear superficially as matters of technique, usually resolve themselves into differences of personal or social attitude, matters of value and belief. Where the four writers we have mentioned differ fundamentally is in the quality of their *insight,* the degree of their sensitive understanding of human experience. And it is precisely this that the critic is anxious to discuss. How can he do so except by reference to his own insight, such as it is? If he is a Christian worthy of the name, his whole outlook will be coloured by his religion; he will see life in Christian terms, and, though he may ignore an atheist writer's professed atheism, he will still judge his degree of insight into character by his own insight, which will have been formed in part by his Christian experience. And the non-Christian critic—let us be clear about

24

this—will also judge a writer's insight into character (or into anything else, of course) by the standard of his own insight, however derived. There
is no 'impartial criticism' in this sense, or rather
there is no critical neutrality; there are only Christian critics and Marxist critics and Moslem critics
—and critics who think themselves disinterested
but who are really swayed unconsciously by the
beliefs they have necessarily acquired by being
members of a particular society in a particular
place and time. The last are really the least impartial, for, believing themselves impartial, they
are open to every unconscious influence upon their
judgement, while the 'doctrinaire' critic may keep
his doctrine well in view and, if not entirely avoid-
ing prejudice, may at least give his readers fair
warning of what to expect. The 'pure critics' of
today adhere in fact to the dogmatic position of
nineteenth-century humanism, which has been
for so long the atmosphere of English academic
circles that it is taken for granted like the air itself.
It postulates a purely human absolute above the
flux of systems and creeds and implies what many
would nowadays regard as an unjustifiably opti-
mistic view of human nature. The Christian, on
the other hand, knows that there is no human way
of transcending the limitations of history, that
human judgements are clouded and partial and
that assumptions, unexamined because scarcely
realized as assumptions, are part of the lot of fallen
man. Such dogma, untrue or unclear, reflects the
curse of Adam, and against it we have only to set
the revealed dogma which we experience as a

partial clearing of vision. With such knowledge of our human plight, the Christian critic has little reason for arrogance, and if he should fail to do justice in his calling the fault lies with him and not the Cause he has espoused.

IV 'Words, words, words'

MACBETH'S OUTBURST ON HEARING of his wife's death is among the most famous of Shakespeare's great speeches:

Tomorrow, and tomorrow, and tomorrow,
Creeps in this petty pace from day to day,
To the last syllable of recorded time;
And all our yesterdays have lighted fools
The way to dusty death. Out, out, brief candle!
Life's but a walking shadow; a poor player,
That struts and frets his hour upon the stage,
And then is heard no more: it is a tale
Told by an idiot, full of sound and fury,
Signifying nothing.

The theme is time, the insignificance of human history. The dragging rhythm of the first three lines, achieved by long vowels, clogging consonants and the extra syllable in the word 'syllable', which cannot in speech be elided, suggests both the hopeless weariness of the speaker and the slow, inevitable advance of time; the explosive labials in 'petty pace' imply disgust. 'Recorded time' hints at the Recording Angel, whose purposeful activity is denied by the speech as a whole; the 'record' is later perverted into an idiotic tale. 'Yesterdays' continues the time theme, but the verb 'lighted' introduces a new, though related, image—the candle, which is used as symbolical of human life,

quickly burning out and easily extinguished. In
his later work Shakespeare's images are usually
functional: he considers the characteristic activity
of the image-object rather than its sensory qualities and is thus closely related to Donne and the
metaphysical poets. The alliterative 'dusty death'
significantly echoes 'day to day', and 'dusty' shows
that Macbeth's imagination does not go beyond
the grave and physical corruption. (The eighteenth-
century emendation, 'dusky', with its suggestion
of Avernus, shows how Shakespeare can be mis-
read by those who bring their own preconceptions
to the task of criticism.) The 'brief candle' emerges
out of 'lighted' and a sequence of related images
follows, each suggested by the one before it: the
'shadow' is cast by candlelight, the 'player' is a
shadow of reality, the 'tale' is the drama of life in
which he plays. A similar chain of images could
be found in surrealistic writing, but without any
meaning beyond itself. Here the imagery is kept
in subordination, being used by the conscious
mind to express a definite judgement; there was a
free passage from unconscious to conscious in
Shakespeare, which to quite an extent accounts
for his greatness. 'Tale' also refers back to 'recorded time', and we are thus given a closely organized presentation—appealing to the whole mind
on every level, not just to the conscious intellect—
of the atheism to which Macbeth has been reduced
by a life of self-centred ambition and sordid crime,
losing his grasp of metaphysical reality, of the
natural and supernatural order, through his per-
sistent pursuit of unnatural ends. Macbeth began

as a convinced Christian. He made his choice of evil deliberately, in the face of heaven, being prepared to 'jump the life to come' and for the sake of worldly ambition to sell his soul to the Devil, his 'eternal jewel . . . to the common enemy of man'. But crime led to crime, free will became replaced by an evil *habitus,* and now, at the end of a career of blood, his soul, shrivelled by sin, with no power left to see things as they are, projects his own internal confusion upon the universe. We must remember the close inter-relation of microcosm and macrocosm in the Elizabethan-Jacobean mind and the relation of both to the body politic. Macbeth really does in outward fact project his own confusion into the body politic—Scotland groans under his oppressive rule—and even, with the help of the witches, into the natural-supernatural order. But evil is essentially negative: it can create only illusion, and Macbeth's half-consoling vision of an evil and purposeless universe is shattered by the triumph of Malcolm, aided by the forces of the holy English king and even more by 'the powers above' who have 'put on their instruments' to vindicate the right. Those who ascribe Macbeth's atheistical opinions to Shakespeare himself have failed to read the play as a whole, which is as necessary as the scrutiny of particular passages.

I have gone into this speech of Macbeth in some detail, not because I want to say anything about Shakespeare just now but in order to provide what I hope is an illustration of modern critical method. I may add that I have also a faint hope that the passage has not already been treated by Dr Leavis, but his work has for so long been digested in my mind that I can never be quite sure that he is not before me; at least I am sure that my emphases are somewhat different from his. My approach differs, also, in its combination of theological considerations with close criticism of the text. It is, however, to the latter that I wish to draw particular attention at present, for such detailed study of the words themselves is the product of a virtual revolution in literary criticism and stands as the foundation principle of modern critical method. In future essays I intend to point out certain limitations inherent in the method and some errors connected with it historically though not logically, but for the moment I am content to profess myself, so far as my abilities allow, a devout practitioner of 'close verbal criticism'. It has long been a commonplace that 'the style is the man himself' but earlier critics habitually ignored the fact. Usually they discussed 'content' in abstraction: plot, character, atmosphere and so forth—and concluded with a hasty remark about the style as 'easy and flowing' or 'adorned with striking epithets'. It was, I believe, Mr T. S. Eliot's *Sacred Wood* that first showed us how a close scrutiny of style—a detailed study of the actual words on the page—might serve to assess a writer's importance or to bring out the significance of a cultural tradition. We began to see the inadequacy of the usual history of literature, an amalgam of biography and history of thought, with inter-chapters on 'prosodic developments'. The true literary history would be primarily a history of the English language as used by the best writers,

which would be found to reflect accurately the cultural history of the nation. It has not yet been
written, and perhaps the new approach to literary
criticism is insufficiently established to produce a
substitute for the *Cambridge History of English
Literature*. The work of Dr Richards and Dr
Leavis did much to make of literary criticism an
intellectual discipline capable of tackling some of
the pressing problems of the contemporary cultural anarchy, especially the detection of the bogus.
Like Nature in the eighteenth, criticism in the
twentieth century became 'methodized'. Of course
there is still no substitute for the old prerequisites:
learning, good manners (a sense of propriety) and,
above all, human feeling and insight. In some of
Dr Leavis's disciples the discipline of criticism
seems to have degenerated into an external technique. This is fatal; there is no merely technical
approach to the words of a poem, and the reactions
of a reader of good will, common sense and ordinary human sympathy are far more worth having
than the most painstaking technical analysis by a
mind devoid of these qualities.

The new axiom, then, is that for the critic 'form'
and 'content' are identical, or that they are only
different ways of looking at the same thing. For in
poetry—and in prose also, though less noticeably
—every change of a word brings about some corresponding change in meaning (e.g., 'dusty' and
'dusky' in the passage from *Macbeth*). It is misleading to think of a writer as 'putting an idea into
words'. Very often he has, strictly speaking, no
'idea' until the words are formulated, but only a

general propulsion, an indistinct shape which has somehow to be realized in words. And even if he has an idea clearly in mind before beginning to write—if Herrick sighed to himself 'Ah, the transience of girlhood's prime!' before a word of 'Gather ye rosebuds' had occurred to him—it is still untrue to say that in making a poem of it he does no more than 'clothe' the idea with words, as if words were an optional drapery. Words are not applied after thinking; they are the means of thought (or *a* means, for it is possible to think in line and colour or in musical sound). So in putting even a preconceived idea into words, the writer is bringing it into active and mutually modifying relationship with a quantity of stored ideas and impressions and emotions: in Herrick's mind girlhood is related to rosebuds and both to happiness and beauty, and for Shakespeare the thought of human life suggests the candle, the theatre and the tale. To the writer himself this integrative process may present itself as 'form' or 'content', as the search for words or as the clarification of ideas, for in the process of composition form and content have not yet coalesced and resistance is experienced sometimes in the definition of attitudes (content) and sometimes in approaching the ideal form which is already vaguely adumbrated. The process of composition may be thought of—a little fantastically perhaps—as the struggle of form and content, neither yet wholly in being, to become themselves by becoming each other; it is not unrelated to love and to mystical experience. In the achieved work form and content are, for better or worse, identical. The content is not just a bare abstraction, the poem's 'message', but the whole tissue of inter-related experience which has evolved, much of it unconsciously, in the course of composition. For a poem is an experience, to the writer and to the reader; it conveys not merely abstract thought but a complex state of mind in which thought and feeling are mutually involved. This complex meaning is attained and expressed through the words in their totality, through their physical properties and associations as well as their dictionary meaning (we have seen something of the importance of rhythm, alliteration, etc., in the speech of Macbeth). Different writers utilize in different ways and to varying degrees the overtones of meaning which words can convey, and their content will vary accordingly: Donne employs 'harsh verse' (his own phrase) for strenuously intellectual poetry, while Spenser and Tennyson more frequently employ a mellifluousness appropriate to their themes. All this will apply to prose also, though here the rational element usually predominates and dictionary meanings are correspondingly more important. An abstract of a poem's meaning is no substitute for the work itself, though with a treatise in philosophy an abstract might give us all we should need to know. Even a philosophical treatise has its overtones of further meaning, but they are not central to its purpose as they are to poetry and some types of 'literary' prose. Poetry is especially satisfying because of its 'density' of meaning (I think the phrase is Dr Leavis's); the meaning addresses itself to every level of the mind

33

C

and, though it may be *apprehended* at time's without conscious effort, can be *analysed* only by a close examination of the words in all their properties. Analysis is not everybody's job, but the reading of sound criticism should enrich our appreciation not only of particular poems but of what poetry is and what it can do for us. Poetry does not merely extend our knowledge; it enlarges our experience of life. And, further, this experience is not presented 'in the raw', but sifted and ordered, implying, if it does not overtly express, an interpretation in terms of meaning and value. Poetry equally with philosophy is an attempt to arrive at the truth, but its method is not abstractive and rational; it throws itself back on the undivided mind, prior to any separation into faculties. It is perhaps that which constitutes its chief fascination for the modern fragmented mind in its search for an organic unity.

V   Levels of Abstraction

W E HAVE SEEN THAT the fundamental process in modern literary criticism is a close
examination of the words themselves.
This is not, however, the only process necessary for
criticism. It is quite true that the words *are* the
poem—or the essay or whatever it is—but it is also
true that, when once the words have mediated to
us the experience that they convey, it is possible to
contemplate and discuss that experience on various
'levels', at various stages or degrees of abstraction.
A purist devotee of the new method hardly regards
as criticism anything which departs from the verbal level. This is mere fanaticism; but it is nevertheless exceedingly dangerous to attempt to discuss
'higher' levels, such as plot, character or thought,
before making quite sure that the verbal level has
been properly assimilated. Take the 'thought' of a
poem for example. The consciously expressed
'philosophy' may be very different from that which
is implied in the unconscious attitudes conveyed
by the style, and to discuss the conscious thought
alone may lead to a complete misunderstanding of
the work. To interpret Pope's *Ethic Epistles* in
terms of his theory of 'the ruling passion', a piece
of crude contemporary psychology which Johnson
roundly and rightly condemns as anti-Christian

and immoral, would be to miss his real moral
standards which are rooted in the Christian tradition (v. his condemnation of the pride and luxury
of Timon's villa and his praise of the Man of Ross).
A real discussion of the question must point to the
muddle in Pope's mind, to the fact that he held an
anti-Christian theory without knowing it to be
anti-Christian and that, although it occasionally
leads him into questionable statements, his good
sense and moral insight usually prevail. The theory
represents Pope's bid to be considered as a thinker;
fortunately he easily forgets it and there is little
harm done. From this example a principle emerges:
it is valuable to consider works of literature on
these higher levels, but they must be true abstractions from the poetic experience as a whole that we
consider, and not false abstractions attained by
isolating only one element of a complex structure.
How this applies to plot and character in Shakespeare I have explained in luxurious detail else-
where. Plot may not usefully be considered apart
from the pattern of themes, and character is often
expressed poetically. Cleopatra is not merely a
royal strumpet, for she has a quality which makes
'defect perfection', a quality which can be expressed only in a divinizing poetic alchemy. Once
this is grasped it is possible to discuss in some
abstraction, though with frequent necessary re-
turns to the text, the quality of her love for Antony
and his for her and to discover that, in Shakespeare's view, far from being the occasion of
Antony's fall, she was in fact his rescuer from 'the
world's great snare', in which the calculating and

ruthless Octavius had been fatally entrapped—a view directly opposite to that which comes from taking the characters solely as they are expressed in action.

When once the words have done their job and the full content of the poem—or what you will—is available to us, we may discuss that content on any level; only, as I said, we must be sure that it is the full content from which we are abstracting. All sorts of interesting themes may be entered upon; for instance we might examine the garden poems of different periods, not for their literary quality but to discover what types of garden were favoured at various times and why. Although this is not itself literary criticism, a good deal of preliminary criticism would be necessary to discover fundamental and representative attitudes, and the task might be crowned by a final comparison of horticultural and poetic styles through the ages. As with the scientist, a negative result in such matters would be as interesting as a high correlation. Shakespeare, Milton and Cowper all enjoy the same country scenes, but Shakespeare and Cowper share rather more than Milton in the farmer's way of seeing them; yet Cowper is nearer to Milton than to Shakespeare in style.

The eighteenth century provides interesting complications in the levels of experience. Renaissance neo-classicism had come into its own, combined not inappropriately with the new scientific outlook which, however modified, derived from classical sources. To the Augustan mind form and content were distinct elements of composition; and

words were regarded as the mere 'dress' of a
thought already clearly apprehended. It was usual
to compare poetry with painting, as Pope does
more than once in the *Essay on Criticism,* and the
poet's words with the painter's colours—in an age,
moreover, when colour was something merely
added to an outline already drawn in. We have
seen in the previous essay that this is a highly misleading account of the process of poetic composition, in which words are the very stuff of thinking.
There is nothing in literature corresponding to
the sheer craft of painting; a poem is a purely mental construction and is, fortunately for some of my
poetic friends, quite independent of penmanship.
Yet this crude theory of composition did influence
the actual practice of Augustan poets; they tended
to draw up a skeleton outline of the poem first and
then to proceed to what they regarded as the more
mechanical task of 'putting it into words'. There
is, of course, no harm in sketching out the main
thought of a poem beforehand—some of our contemporaries might benefit from the practice—and
there is no harm in adopting a comparatively 'external' and craftsmanlike approach to the act of
composition. Some writers are by nature spontaneous and unselfconscious, while others practise
their art with calculated effect; each type has its
own virtues and defects. For the Augustans the
harm lay in thinking of the general conception as
'inspired' and its expression as relatively mechanical. Thus the actual process of composition, which
is the 'putting into words,' tended to become less
personal than it had been in the previous century,

and the choice of words and images less an inevitable crystallization from the unconscious in the course of defining a meaning or seeking the ideal form and more a deliberate search for phrases appropriate to the canons of contemporary taste. The poet drew not so much on his own stored impressions as on a common pool of favourite images and 'turns', often derived from the 'Ancients'. Pope himself, though subscribing to current literary beliefs and practice, was too great a poet to be bound by them; their effect is more clearly seen in the relative poverty of minor Augustan verse after the minor poetry of the seventeenth century.

How are we to approach such poetry? With our own method in which form and content are treated as identical or with the Augustan categories? Certainly with our own method first, if we are to understand just what is the peculiar quality of Augustan poetry, for from our point of view the Augustan split between 'form' and 'content' is itself a part of the full content. The various subsidiary aims additional to that of adequate poetic expression—the aesthetic pleasure to be gained from smooth and regular verse, the imitation of the Ancients, the adherence to prescribed rules of composition—are an important part of the full meaning of Augustan poetry, expressing the artificial elegance and studied propriety of the age. When once this is perceived there is no harm in going on to play the game of Augustan criticism, speaking of the general conception and then of particular stylistic graces, in order to appreciate

the writer's technical skill by seeing from his point
of view the difficulties he had to overcome; but it
takes the modern method (and Dr Leavis) to show
how much of Pope's superiority comes from a deep
affinity with the metaphysical tradition. Johnson
condemns and Bloomsbury praises the Sporus portrait as an exhibition of spiteful fury, but a close
verbal scrutiny of image and symbol will reveal it
as an excellent poetic statement of metaphysical
evil, and its immediate occasion scarcely matters.
Sporus is 'one vile antithesis'. His character is in-
troduced by the paradoxical query: 'Who breaks
a butterfly upon a wheel?', and the mounting conceits develop in balanced terms: he is a *'bug* with
gilded wings', a *'painted* child of *dirt'*, then later a
'familiar toad' 'at the ear of Eve'. Here the phrase
seems to mean little more than a 'toady', a syco-
phantic courtier breathing his suggestions into a
female ear, presumably that of Queen Caroline;
the strong hint of Eden and the Fall lies somewhat
in the background, but at the climax, a few lines
later, becomes explicit in the full identification of
Sporus with the Devil:

> *Eve's tempter thus the Rabbins have express'd,*
> *A cherub's face, a reptile all the rest,*
> *Beauty that shocks you, parts that none will trust,*
> *Wit that can creep, and pride that licks the dust.*

It may not be strictly fair to Lord Hervey, but
surely Pope has left him behind. Sporus is the
devil in us all, with the shocking beauty of God's
creation perverted from its end. Re-reading the
passage, we have leisure to observe in detail the
regularity of the closed couplets and trace the

varying caesura, to distinguish the types of balanced phrase and to pause upon the triplet exactly expressing the instability of its theme:

> *His wit all see-saw, between that and this,*
> *Now high, now low, now master up, now miss,*
> *And he himself one vile antithesis.*

In the average Augustan writer we should admire these graces for themselves, as the necessary medium of polite communication. In Pope, of course, the integration is complete; the coolness and order are essential to the statement: the author is not screaming in uncontrolled fury, as we so often are told, but he dominates his material and directs his fiery shafts with cool calculation. It is this further paradox, the combination of extreme heat and extreme coldness in the writer, which makes possible the universalizing by which a lampoon has grown into a metaphysical poem. With the Augustans, then, two critical approaches are valid at different stages—and the theological or philosophical critic would develop on a more abstract plane the relation between the quasi-scientific separation of form and content and the contemporary growth of scientific rationalism and incipient utilitarianism in the English deists and the French *philosophes*. The exaltation of a false Reason, the deification of a crude scientific method, comes of that breakdown of organic thinking, referred to by Mr Eliot as a 'dissociation of sensibility', which may perhaps best be studied in the change from metaphysical to Augustan poetry.

Another aspect of eighteenth-century literature, its 'pre-romantic' interest in the 'Gothick', illus-

trates a further complication of the levels or degrees of abstraction. Literary revolutions sometimes affect style and subject-matter together, as
with Donne and Mr T. S. Eliot; sometimes they
are primarily stylistic, as with Euphuism or the
mediaeval 'aureate' style (i.e., there is change
of content on the lowest level, necessarily, with
the change of form, but there is not necessarily any
change of subject and ideas); and sometimes they
change the subject-matter without at first any
notable effect upon style. The last is, I think, the
healthiest, since it shows a primary concern for
something outside art itself and allows the art to
become slowly and naturally accommodated to its
new material, as the latter seeps down from conscious to unconscious and from being merely an
interest becomes finally a mode of thinking and
feeling, a new way of experiencing reality. It was
so with the cult of the Gothic: three-quarters of a
century of interest in ruins and armour and spooks,
old ballads and Celtic and Norse mythology, combined with an equally slow rediscovery of some
aspects of external nature, preceded the development of the Romantic style in the early nineteenth
century. In the eighteenth, we are often con-
fronted with romantic subject-matter expressed
in the abstract, balanced manner of neo-classical
prose and verse, as in Gray's poetic excursions into
Celtic and Norse antiquities, in Walpole's *Otranto*
and in the novels of Mrs Radcliffe. No doubt contemporaries did not notice the neo-classicism of
style; they were accustomed to it and accepted it
without thought as the only natural means of com-

munication. So they thrilled to the strange, new romantic material without any sense of incongruity. From our point of view, however, the poetic diction of Gray—ornate and *recherché* to Johnson, but to us more like than unlike Pope in, say, the *Eloisa to Abelard* or the Homer—and the cool, balanced and frequently didactic, though often sentimental, periods of Mrs Radcliffe seem ludicrously out of keeping with the eeriness they attempt to communicate. Once again the examination of style is a necessary beginning, for the true content of an eighteenth-century would-be romantic is not just the Nordic gloom or Celtic twilight of his favourite studies; it is that plus the orderly, commonsensical eighteenth-century daylight attitude to things, which is expressed in his style. His mental processes fall naturally into this rational organization, either because he is an ordinary eighteenth-century gentleman in ordinary life, governed by reason and common sense, and only a sentimental 'enthusiast' in his leisure hours, or because, whatever he may be in himself, the social *milieu* is stronger than he and has stamped itself deep into those layers of the mind that lie beyond his conscious control. It is only with the Romantic Movement proper that we come upon a set of poets who *think* romantically, in whom the normal modes of experience have been modified by romantic preconceptions and whose style is consequently novel and at first repellent to their contemporaries. Such an essentially sociological observation emerges from examining the text of our pre-romantic and romantic writers. We may, indeed, usefully retire to higher levels and study the growth of feeling for the Gothic or the rise of the Satanic hero, but it is safer to do so after the social background has been established by the method of close verbal criticism.

So far we have considered instances in which the higher levels may be interesting but never quite so rewarding as the lower. Are there not others where little need be said about the lower levels and where the main interest is to be found 'higher up'? My answer to this question I must defer until another occasion.

VI   *Narrative*

W HETHER IN VERSE OR prose, dramatic or
non-dramatic, narrative presents a special problem for the critic. Other types
of literature, as we have seen, directly express—
indeed *are*—the writer's thought and feeling. (I do
not say that they express his personality or mood,
since the best poetry is relatively objective and
impersonal, an experience transcending the individual outlook of the writer.) But with narrative
the thought and feeling communicated by the
words serve to recreate in the reader's mind a
sequence of events—the story—and it is to this
sequence of events that the reader responds with
a further pattern of thought and feeling which is
the true end-product of the process. The movement is not straight across (writer to reader) but
across, upward (to the fictional world) and then
down again, and the most significant level, where
the mind lingers, is not the verbal but the ideational—the final response is to events imaginatively recreated, not to word-meanings. The barest
account of some events, a 'stop press' column in
the newspaper, may arouse the passions; the emotive properties of words—sound, rhythm, associa-
tion, imagery—are not absolutely essential, though
to varying degrees they are employed in all literary

45

narrative, their function being the strictly subordinate one of assisting the reader's imaginative reconstruction of the story. All this may seem rather remote, but it has important consequences which concern both the writer and the critic, since here at length we are faced with a situation in which one of the 'higher' levels of abstraction, the story level, is more significant than the verbal level to which modern criticism pays so much attention.

I am quite aware that in roughly dividing literature into narrative and non-narrative I have not exhausted its possibilities; there are *genres* which in defiance of logic seem to combine the two. What are we to say of *Macbeth* or *The Waste Land*? The latter is easier to deal with: it has narrative elements but these are symbolic and illustrative, subordinate to the main theme; the reader's attention is not focused on the story level. With Shakespeare the story is in one sense the main thing: there would be no play without it; but at least in his later works the subtle poetry serves not so much to advance the story as to define his attitudes to it, and it is with these attitudes that we are most concerned. In each instance, then, the narrative element weaves into our response, yet the main response (*pace* a good many Shakespeareans) is to the poetry as poetry—it is on the verbal level. *Twelfth Night* and some other middle-period plays are perhaps rather nearer to true narrative. It is evident that we must distinguish between narrative proper and pseudo-narrative. We must distinguish also between this pseudo-narrative and the experimental narrative of Joyce's *Ulysses* and the novels of

Virginia Woolf, which attempt to tell a story but
on a lower plane of consciousness from that on
which events are usually recorded. It is perhaps
too early to say whether words can satisfactorily
do that sort of thing—whether they can be made
to represent a 'low' level of consciousness any more
immediately than by the normal method of abstract
statement. My own feeling is that the unconscious
cannot be consciously expressed without changing
its nature and that the only true expression of the
unconscious is that which is unconsciously implied
in ordinary conscious statements.

Returning to the question of straightforward
narrative prose and verse, we may ask precisely
what the critic will discover by a close examination
of the words and how far such an examination will
take him towards an assessment of value. We have
seen that the main function of the words is to establish the story as an imaginative creation in the
reader's mind. In this connection we may consider
the style as abstract or concrete, sparing or luxu-
riant in description, etc., and all this tells us something of the writer. Other matters also may become
clear from the style: the writer's attitude to his
subject and his attitude to the reader, 'feeling' and
'tone' in the terminology of Dr Richards. The verbal level may not be central or final but it is highly
important and, particularly by critics of the novel,
it has been unduly neglected in the past. Some
years ago, in the last days of the old *Criterion*, I
attempted to trace the development of George
Eliot as a novelist almost entirely by examining
passages from her different works in chronological

order. It was possible to show an advance from the rather sentimental *Scenes of Clerical Life* to the taut, intellectual and often satiric prose of *Middlemarch* and *Daniel Deronda;* the quality of mind had improved with age and experience and this was evident in the style itself. I incline to think that a similar study of Dickens' style would be equally revealing, but critics have usually preferred to discuss him in terms of social reform and England's wayside inns. The attitude to the reader is highly important: Fielding's irritating superiority, especially in the over-praised introductory chapters, makes him less pleasant company than Smollett, whose good manners and greater interest in the yarn for its own sake usually prevented him from buttonholing the reader with a moral or literary discourse. Some novelists respond very well to criticism on the verbal level; it takes us a long way, though it is—quite literally—never the whole story. My own views have altered considerably since the days of my essay on George Eliot; what I wrote remains true, I think, but it is not the whole truth. I would still back *Middlemarch* against all the rest as undoubtedly her finest work, but there is something in what the older critics said: the earlier works, *Adam Bede* and *The Mill on the Floss* especially, have a freshness and ease which are not found in her later writings; these qualities exist, however, more on the story level, in the invention, than in the style. Sometimes there is loss in sheer narrative power with the increase in intellectual perception; the critic must weigh the one against the other.

An examination of the style always tells us something; with Fielding, Jane Austen, Dickens and George Eliot it tells us a great deal. But with some novelists we learn little more than that we are not to waste our time on this verbal level. Even such matters as increasing depth of insight need not show themselves in the words—that is to say, they need not appear in the detailed organization of thought and feeling; the prose may remain over abstract and perhaps clumsy, yet there may be great penetration in the treatment of character, incident and thought. This can be understood by recalling my remark in a previous essay about the philosophical treatise, which we are concerned to understand only on a certain level of abstraction. A philosopher is not a good philosopher in direct proportion to his literary ability; he may think boldly and clearly on the main issue without ever bringing the outlying regions of his mind into subjection to his abstractly reasoned thesis. Reading him, we follow the chain of reasoning and ignore so far as possible the tangled undergrowth in which it lies. Similarly with the novelist. It is possible to be a good novelist with an undistinguished or even a poorish style, provided that it is adequate to convey a sequence of events and to delineate the characters who take part in them. Because the reader is concentrating not on the verbal but on the ideational level, he can ignore the style when once he has grown accustomed to it and even supply some of its defects from his own resources. If, for example, the style is imprecise in description, this will not greatly matter unless

49

D

description should somehow become of special
moment for the story. The reader will either grow
accustomed to this sort of poverty or will, quite
unconsciously, supply the requisite imagery himself. Defects of feeling and tone are more serious,
but we can accommodate ourselves even to a senti-
mentalist or a snob if he has something interesting
to say. Most novelists, I suppose, are merely undistinguished in style; their minds do not seek for
that fine clarification of focus which is the special
function of the poet. They are content to accept
their words ready made from the hands of society,
without seeking to squeeze more meaning out of
them or to order them in specially significant ways.
No doubt they have their individual touches, but
it is essentially the style in common literary use
that they employ. Smollett, Scott, Trollope, would
all come under this head; so would Charlotte M.
Yonge. Unless he can write very well in an unos-
tentatious and perfectly translucent prose, it is an
advantage to the novelist not to be a stylist at all,
not to be concerned with the verbal level, since if
the reader's attention is too closely drawn to that
level he is hindered in his progress up and on to
the plane on which the story is unfolded. In the
style of such a writer as Scott the virtues and vices
are primarily those of the period and a knowledge
of them contributes more to sociology or the history of civilization than to an understanding of his
individual significance; for that we must go to
another level, where in Scott we should remark the
sense of tradition, his unfailing habit of seeing
every age in relation to the ages preceding it,

so that even in a contemporary novel like *The Antiquary* the strata of history lie revealed.

The critic of narrative has a complex task. His final verdict cannot be reached on the verbal level, but on this level there is nevertheless much to be done. Primarily he must see whether the style impedes or facilitates the reader's process of imaginatively recreating the story. Story-telling must set up and sustain an illusion of reality (which, of course, has nothing to do with realism) and anything in the style which draws attention to itself is an interference with its own proper function. Shakespeare keeps his audience critically alert and constantly aware of the play as a play; this is because he is not any more exercised about dramatic illusion than is a modern writer of musical comedy; his art works in another way. There is an element of illusion, but this is repeatedly broken through to convey an active *poetic* 'criticism of life' for which the real world must be co-present with the play world in the minds of his audience. With Shakespeare it is what he brings to the story that matters, whereas the true story-teller's criticism of life shapes itself within the succession of events. The best narrative verse comes from simple ages, where the style is unindividual: Homer, *Beowulf*, the ballads and the Spanish romances—or it is found in deliberate and often pseudo-archaic simplifications, like the *Idylls of the King* and a good deal of Morris. The 'metaphysical' tradition is hopeless for narrative, as we can see from *Annus Mirabilis;* eighteenth-century poetic diction is better when once you are accustomed to it: its very

51

expectedness is an advantage. Some modern novelists should be warned against an excess of similes: Dickens uses them well but sparingly (those formidable mittens that always suggested a meat-safe); if the page is littered with similes, they produce a kaleidoscopic jumble which interferes with visuallizing or with whatever the non-visualizers do instead. And they draw attention away from the story to that smart fellow, the author. An author's appearances in the first person should be few and well managed, for they always break the imaginative sequence. There are no rules; it is a matter of tact. Dickens is more successful here than Fielding, perhaps because of that very fellow-feeling for his characters which renders him suspect in some quarters. We have already seen that the social implications of style must be considered; a good storyteller may suffer considerably through accepting uncritically the social idiom of a bad period. Matters of 'feeling' and 'tone' may also call for investigation; but work on the verbal level is chiefly negative, detecting what interferes with the author's real job. After these preliminaries the critic moves on to the story level with the consideration of plot, character and thought. This is his main task, but I need discuss it no further, since critical methods at that level are well known and their results generally appreciated.

VII   *Two Streams from Helicon*

I—CHARACTERISTICS

IT HAS MORE THAN once been suggested to me,
by reviewers and other well-wishers, that critical canons founded upon theology must necessarily be wanting in that catholicity with a small
'c' which should be the aim of every literary critic. I
have previously shown that I do not intend a writer
to be judged by his professed dogmatic position but
by what I have called the quality of his insight, and
the only touchstone that we possess for such a judgement is the quality of our own insight, which will be
modified by our Christianity if we are Christians,
our Marxism if we are Marxists, our naturalism if
we are naturalistic humanists. In other words, there
are no purely literary judgements, just as there are
no purely economic judgements; we cannot isolate
one aspect of human activity from all the rest and
make a comfortable, self-contained 'subject' or
'science' of it. We are dealing with a universe,
ABC, and we cannot really know A if we ignore B
and C. Economics is not a 'pure' science; it is involved with matters of ethics, politics, biology and
so forth: literary criticism is not a 'pure' activity,
since literature is a cultural expression and its
boundaries are as wide as life. We cannot have it
both ways: if literature is more than a pleasant pas-
time played according to certain rules, if its breadth

is the breadth of human experience, then it is fraught with all the uncertainties of human experience and the great controversies about the meaning of life will all be reflected in our literary criticism. In founding literary judgements upon theology we are granting the catholicity of literature and at the same time postponing general agreement upon it until Judgement Day. But we at least know approximately where we stand and are less a prey to the unconscious prejudices of that ambiguous entity, an open mind. The recent history of literary criticism shows that when no fixed standards are adopted, exterior to the art itself, the result is the very reverse of the catholicity which is admittedly so desirable. For standards of a sort seem to be natural to man: he must set something up and trample something down in the necessary exercise of his discrimination. And if he will not admit exterior standards, he adopts interior standards which are more exclusive.

Speaking very broadly, we may say that there are two main types of English poetry, that represented *par excellence* by Shakespeare and Donne (to which it has been customary to add, very doubtfully to my mind, the name of Hopkins and, less doubtfully, that of Mr Eliot) and the other great stream represented by such key figures as Spenser, Milton and Tennyson. Abstract descriptions of 'types' of poetry are never very satisfactory, yet they can be useful: what follows is an attempt to draw a general distinction, pressed to ideal limits, between these two great poetic streams.

(*a*) The *language* of the Shakespeare-Donne type

is founded on the colloquial speech of the day
('Busie old foole, unruly Sunne'), whereas that of
the others is relatively a special creation for poetic
purposes: Spenser's antique, Chaucerian air, Milton's Latinity, Tennyson's occasional archaism and
his pervasive 'romantic' colour. For the former the
language of poetry is essentially that of ordinary
life; for the latter there is a special 'poetic' tradition with its own sort of vocabulary. In Shakespeare, too, we find this special poetic vocabulary,
with the rhetorical figures appropriate to it, but
the fundamental and dominant strain is colloquial.
Again, Shakespeare and Donne will employ harsh
or sweet-sounding combinations of words, whichever best reinforce their meaning, whereas with
the others (not so much with Milton, perhaps) the
tendency is to produce a general effect of sweetness
and smoothness. Shakespeare will hiss to convey
the sinister brooding of Macbeth:

> . . . *if th' assassination*
> *Could trammel up the consequence, and catch,*
> *With his surcease, success*—

while Tennyson deliberately reduced the number
of sibilants in his lines. Whereas Shakespeare and
Donne are entirely concerned for the optimum expression of meaning (for them Truth is Beauty), the
Spenser-Milton-Tennyson tradition has a dual purpose: to convey a meaning and also 'to please' by a
sustained and relatively 'exterior' aesthetic appeal.
This must, however, be distinguished from the
Augustan exteriority, with its theory of imitation,
its rigid rules and consequently limited range.

(*b*) There is a similar and nearly related contrast

in *rhythm*. Shakespeare and Donne are not closely
bound to metrical regularity: they seem, as it were,
to counterpoint their metre with the rhythms of
speech; we are aware of the metrical pattern
but the speech-pattern is superimposed upon it.
Donne's strenuosity has been commented on since
Coleridge's epigram: he 'wreathes iron pokers into
true-love knots'. The well-worn instance from
Satire III: 'On a huge hill,/Cragged, and steep,
Truth stands'—has been overworked as an example
of Donne's manner, yet it is hardly representative.
It was understood by the Elizabethans that all
satire must be 'rough', after the model of Persius,
and, moreover, this particular passage has an experimental quality different even from the general
run of the satires, though there are other sections
comparable to it and they seem to have inspired
the wayward genius of Benlowes later. *Aire and
Angels* provides a more characteristic example of
Donne's speech-rhythm:

> *Ev'ry thy haire for love to worke upon*
> *Is much too much, some fitter must be sought;*
> *For, nor in nothing, nor in things*
> *Extreme, and scatt'ring bright, can love inhere.*

Transferred stresses and packed consonants account for the prosodic variety; though speech-
rhythm is dominant, the metre is regular enough.
Here and in most of his verse Donne differs from
other poets only in doing much more often what
all of them do from time to time. There is plenty
of rhythmic variety in the Spenser-Milton-Tennyson tradition, but the effect is not contrapuntal;
variety is achieved by a subtle introduction of

speech accents which leaves the metrical pattern dominant, as can be seen in those justly famous lines of Tennyson:

> *Music that gentlier on the spirit lies,*
> *Than tir'd eyelids upon tir'd eyes,*

where the effect is obtained by the dragging 'i' sounds and the absence of stress on the third foot in the second line.

(*c*) The contrast is maintained in the use of *imagery*. (I employ the term loosely to include direct description as well as simile and metaphor.) In Shakespeare and Donne imagery is essentially functional; it is a principal means of thinking, and the image-object is chosen less for its pictorial and aesthetic quality than for its intellectual significance. It follows that a wider range of imagery is open to this type of poet. In Shakespeare the tendency is for one image to run into another; a successful reading demands that they should be realized clearly with the intellect but somewhat hazily in their sensory properties: 'Was the hope drunk/Wherein you drest yourself?' (The abstract hope is personified as drunk and then immediately becomes a suit of clothes.) Donne's conceits are more self-conscious and clearly defined and the purely intellectual element is even stronger: 'Thinke thy shell broke, thinke thy Soule hatch'd but now', i.e., at death, which is thus regarded as a new and truer birth. They can, however, carry a great deal of aesthetic and atmospheric suggestion, as in *Aire and Angels* and the *Nocturnall upon S. Lucies day*, but this is always subordinate to the main intellectual purpose. Imagery in Spenser,

Milton and Tennyson is much more pictorial and descriptive in aim and aesthetic and 'romantic' in quality. Yet at the same time—and this is something of a paradox—it tends to be more general, subjective, emotive. Milton never provides a clear, objective description; he is no Dutch painter, much more an impressionist. He projects emotion: in 'That glorious form, that light unsufferable', the epithets are general and suggest no defined objective 'picture', only the emotional response. The negative 'unsufferable' is quite typical; he frequently builds up by baffled negatives a whole grand scene which would defy direct description:

> Before their eyes in sudden view appear
> The secrets of the hoary Deep—a dark
> Illimitable ocean, without bound,
> Without dimension; where length, breadth, and highth,
> And time, and place, are lost . . .

For all his classicism he is the great romantic, filled with the mystery of the remote, the unfathomed, the far border-country of the mind:

> . . . or who with Saturn old
> Fled over Adria to the Hesperian fields,
> And o'er the Celtic roamed the utmost Isles.

Of course Shakespeare has this in abundance and Donne is not without it: there is a romantic folklore quality in the song 'Goe, and catche a falling starre', which stands in characteristic contrast to its main purport, a witty indictment of inconstancy in woman. But Donne remains as the perfect opposite to Milton and, though Shakespeare, like his own Feste, is 'for all waters' and both streams flow into that boundless sea, in his general treatment of language, rhythm and imagery, he must certainly be regarded as the chief tributary of our first stream.

(*d*) Leaving the more technical matters of language, etc., our two groups provide a further interesting set of contrasts. In *subject-matter* Group A (the Shakespeare-Donne group) is more contemporary; even when Shakespeare sets his story in the remote past he is actively concerned with contemporary issues. Group B casts a romantic halo over the past: Spenser's paladins and Tennyson's Round Table fit well with Milton's

> *. . . faery damsels met in forest wide*
> *By knights of Logres, or of Lyones,*
> *Lancelot, or Pelleas, or Pellenore.*

Another paradox. In *general approach* Group A are more spontaneous, less studied: Shakespeare's copies, notoriously free from 'blots', testify to his rapidity and ease of composition, and in reading the works of his maturity one cannot help feeling that, however closely he thought out the matter of his plays, it must have organized itself into appropriate words with little conscious effort. Donne gives the same impression: he did not much study his 'art' or 'craft'; his mind must have focused on the level of ideas, leaving the words to tumble spontaneously into place. Undoubtedly he has moments of technical experiment, but the more pervasive rhetorical patterns would have become second nature in one of his learning. Group B are conscious artists; they work more 'from the outside'. Words are deliberately chosen; at times, indeed, Milton seems to be making a language for

59

himself and Spenser does a little in the same way. Yet—and here lies the paradox—Group A are very much more controlled, sophisticated, alert, subtle, assured, in *tone*. They have a self-awareness which causes them to say no more than they would wish to say. Donne the lover himself mentions his palsy, his gout and his five grey hairs; if his youthful ardour should appear slightly ridiculous to the on-looker, the latter is required to note that it appears slightly ridiculous to himself also. Milton is less secure: the fallen angels in the first two books of *Paradise Lost* have a strong Commonwealth flavour and his Eve, while yet unfallen, is embar-rassingly luscious and coy. The truth is that the conscious artist, working from outside, is so occu-pied with technical matters that certain undesired elements in his subject-matter can slip past uncen-sored; the more spontaneous writer concentrates at a different level and is more careful of what he says. Again, Group A, being wholly occupied with thought, usually produces 'difficult' poetry; the poetry of Group B, where the concentration is upon 'art', is a great deal simpler.

It is almost inexcusable to pot a criticism of Eng-lish poetry in a few paragraphs as I have attempted to do, but I think that the reader will hold me justified in distinguishing the two streams that I have briefly explored. Now there are some writers, among them Dr Leavis, who at least imply that Group A are doing the right things, while Group B are essentially wrong. This is the internal dis-crimination of which I have complained. Dr Leavis has always conceded the genius of Milton

(I do not think that he has said very much about Spenser and Tennyson) but he has deplored the Miltonic style and even more the influence that Milton has exercised on succeeding poets. Here I partly agree, but it seems none the less dangerous to hail the Shakespeare-Donne type of thing as the genuine English tradition and, even if tacitly, to consign that other great tradition to some limbo of false aims and deluded aspiration. Why has this drastic judgement been passed and what is the real truth of the matter? As in my youth the film 'serials' used to leave us with the screaming heroine chained to the old mill-wheel, so I must leave these important questions for another fortnight.

II—The Argument from Tradition

Last time, I attempted to bring out the differences between two great streams of English poetry: Group A, the Shakespeare-Donne type, and Group B, the Spenser-Milton-Tennyson type. I should like again to emphasize the fact that I am pressing the distinction to ideal limits. In reality every poet has some of the characteristics of each group; Shakespeare especially combines all the characteristics of both, though we have seen reason to consider him primarily as the chief figure in Group A. And I must also make quite clear that in saying that Dr Leavis and his fellow-workers in *Scrutiny* consider Group A to be fun-

damentally right and Group B wrong, I have no
intention of suggesting that their criticism con-
sists in a crude adherence to one poetic party. The
fineness of discrimination, the scrupulous care
which Dr Leavis himself invariably exercises,
naturally prohibits any such easy verdict. I refer
merely to a tendency to approve the essential
Group A qualities and look askance upon those of
Group B. If a Group B poet is praised it is rather
for his occasional display of Group A qualities
than for his true characteristics, as an unusually
'Jacobean' speech of Comus is praised, for example, in an essay by Dr Leavis on Milton's style.
I promised my patient readers a fortnight ago that
I should attempt this time an answer to the questions with which I left them: Why do certain
modern critics set up, as it were, the Group A type
of poetry against the Group B, and what should
be our attitude to these very different approaches
to the poet's task? But I find I have entered deep
waters and it will take me some considerable time
to win my way to the farther shore. For the present
I shall content myself with considering one point
in isolation.

If I am not mistaken, it is sometimes suggested
that Group A represents to a special degree the
native English poetic tradition. I cannot myself
agree that this is so. Admittedly Shakespeare and
Donne resisted Renaissance neo-classicism in some
directions. Shakespeare ignored the 'Aristotelian'
rules of drama but none the less absorbed much of
the classical matter and the classical aesthetic attitudes which the age pressed upon him; the sheer

beauty of his poetry, in the obvious sense of the word, is a gift of the Renaissance. Donne rejected smooth numbers, 'clarity', and the accessories of pagan mythology, but Persius is his model in satire and Ovid has influenced his discarding of the Petrarchan tradition. If we are to search for origins, there is something of the strenuosity of Shakespeare and Donne in *Beowulf* and Old English poetry generally, but there is also a conventional poetic diction quite alien to the colloquial idiom of the Jacobeans, and the emotive-pictorial imagery and lofty dignity of tone are nearer Milton than Donne; indeed it has been suspected that Milton studied that grand *Genesis* fragment which describes the fall of the angels—its account of hell, their *dimman hām*, can bear comparison with the opening of *Paradise Lost*. 'Poetic diction', if we may use the term broadly to signify a specially selected language for poetic use, originates in simple times, where the poet is accounted a seer and words have quasi-magical powers; naturally in such times the poet speaks in a voice different from that of other men. Virgil's poetic diction is consciously derived, part of his joint effort with Augustus to revive the Heroic Age. Milton, too, is consciously 'heroic', deliberately placing himself third in the line of great English poets; Chaucer and Spenser, his predecessors, had both in their way maintained through a special poetic vocabulary the high calling of the bard. Eighteenth-century poetic diction, to which the term is usually restricted, suffers from being too close an imitation of the Virgilian imitation; its mannered surface concealed an increasing intellectual and social disintegration but was bound itself to disintegrate under the pressure of cultural change. Wordsworth's reform, however, was less thorough than he thought and his later work tacitly repudiates the extremes of the *Lyrical Ballads,* which themselves are only sporadically colloquial in diction and seldom in rhythm and word-order. In general the Romantics still employ a sort of poetic diction and this is continued with modifications by Tennyson and the Pre-Raphaelites: it is more various and less Latinized than the diction of eighteenth-century poetry; archaism takes the place of Latinity; but it is almost equally remote from the language of every day. Poetic diction, then, is continuous in the 'bardic' tradition of English poetry, the Group B tradition which significantly preserves in its regular, incantatory rhythms and emotive-pictorial suggestion something of the wonder and awe, the numinous borderland experience which harks back to our primitive ancestry. Poetry of this kind plays on the general, fundamental human emotions; it has a quality of high simplicity about it and is subtle and ambiguous only in evoking the essential mystery of life and death and the multiple worlds of the imagination.

Colloquial diction, on the other hand, is usually sophisticated; it implies the questioning of social conventions and the repudiation of the bardic tradition. It is therefore found in the early seventeenth century, a period of profound intellectual and social reconstruction, and in the twentieth century, a period of intellectual scepticism and social disintegration. Mediaeval colloquialism is a different phenomenon. In Langland and the writers of the miracle plays it is a social accident: they are not in any assured *literary* tradition and had no other language at command. The difference from Donne is shown in the way they will use the loftier phrase whenever they can, while the miracle writers chop up their verses, like the Wordsworth of the *Lyrical Ballads,* with no regard for the rhythms and word-order of speech. The remarkable poet of *The Owl and the Nightingale,* however, has nothing ingenuous about him: his colloquialism is continuous, surely deliberate, and full of sophisticated wit; if it were not for the difficult dialect one might imagine oneself, reading his terse octosyllabic couplets, in a corner of the early seventeenth century. But, biologically speaking, the author of *The Owl and the Nightingale* is something of a 'sport'. Chaucer, of course, has colloquial turns but in his smooth and regular verse they are skilfully blended with poetic diction. He is best compared with Pope, since both combine fastidious art with a highly civilized use of contemporary idiom; in the latest and best work of each, deft conversational passages, in the word-order and with the easy tone of conversation, are to be found closely incorporated with passages of mock heroic—and all in verse of the strictest regularity: cf. the *Nonne Preestes Tale* and the *Epistle to Dr Arbuthnot.* Spenser modelled himself upon Chaucer in language and Milton had Chaucer frequently in mind. It is true that what we might call —in a limiting though not in any derogatory sense

65

—the half-educated, semi-folk tradition of Langland and the miracle plays did survive through the sixteenth century in the miracles themselves and through the seventeenth century and beyond in the form of ballads, folk-songs and carols. And Dr L. C. Knights has recently shown it cropping up even in the learned and courtly George Herbert, quondam Public Orator in the University of Cambridge —which is not really surprising, since the seventeenth-century gentleman and scholar knew the countryside and its people, particularly when he happened to be a village parson. But by Herbert the proverbial phrases and folk idioms are *used*— deliberately and in verse which, though it has its knotty moments appropriate to the themes of mental strife, is normally fairly smooth and always of a metrical regularity such as Ben Jonson advocated. It would be easy to exaggerate the continuity which the presence of these folk elements suggests. Folk poetry and learned poetry continued side by side with little interchange. Herbert owes nothing directly to mediaeval writers and little to the contemporary ballad, but as a conscientious parson he was familiar with the way his parishioners thought and spoke; from his prose treatise, *A Priest to the Temple,* we know how he studied the rural mind in order to be 'understanded of the people' and it is this which is reflected in his verse. Donne, Crashaw, Vaughan, Marvell, have no trace of the folk tradition.

Perhaps enough has been said to show that on historical grounds there is no reason to regard Group A as in any special degree representative of 'the English tradition'; the claim of Group B is probably stronger. Group A's claim could be maintained only by arguing that the very fact of its colloquial diction links it especially to the 'folk', but this would be to establish not a poetic tradition but a speech tradition—I imagine that the whole business may have originated in a confusion of this kind. Poetic language is 'not necessarily the language of the people; historically there are different degrees of affinity between them. And 'poetic diction', let me insist again, is not the work of scholarly poetic amateurs; it is a fact of primitive society which has never quite lost its hold on succeeding generations.

III—THE POET'S TASK

More serious than the argument from tradition, already considered, is the claim that in the poetry of Group A (the Shakespeare-Donne type) words are being used to their fullest capacity, whereas in Group B (the Spenser-Milton-Tennyson type) they are not. Various metaphors are used to convey this notion: the poetry of Group A is spoken of as 'concrete', 'immediate', the words 'do what they say'. In a sense this claim is just. Colloquial language, because it has the associations of actual use, permits great subtlety of tone in treating human and human-divine relationships; free, rough rhythms allow the words to be so ordered that their sounds combine

into active stresses and strains which may reinforce
the urgent process of impassioned thought; and
functional imagery in its wide range brings together in an intellectual and emotional fusion the
multiple worlds of human discourse. The four-
teenth of Donne's *Holy Sonnets* provides an excellent illustration:

> *Batter my heart, three person'd God; for, you*
> *As yet but knocke, breathe, shine, and seeke to mend;*
> *That I may rise, and stand, o'erthrow mee,' and bend*
> *Your force, to breake, blowe, burn and make me new.*
> *I, like an usurpt towne, to' another due,*
> *Labour to' admit you, but Oh, to no end,*
> *Reason your viceroy in mee, mee should defend,*
> *But is captiv'd, and proves weake or untrue.*
> *Yet dearely' I love you,' and would be loved faine,*
> *But am betroth'd unto your enemie:*
> *Divorce mee,' untie, or breake that knot againe;*
> *Take mee to you, imprison mee, for I*
> *Except you' enthrall mee, never shall be free,*
> *Nor ever chast, except you ravish mee.*

The first line has concentrated force, its desperate
petition strengthened by hard open vowels in 'Batter' and 'heart' and by the 't's', 'r's' and the opening 'b'. This 'b' is taken up in line 4 with the alliterative series of verbs which all refer to destructive processes: 'breake, blowe, burn'. Between
lines 3 and 4 the words truly 'do what they say':

> *o'erthrow mee,' and bend*
> *Your force.*

The 'mee' is an extra syllable, technically elided
before 'and', but we never really elide in English:
it brings out the strain of overthrowing, while
the line-end gap between 'bend' and 'Your force'

68

seems to enact the difficulty of the operation. There is no need to continue this; we have sufficiently noted the use of physical force in the words to strengthen meaning. (There is also a corresponding softness as in 'breathe, shine, and seeke to mend'.) Let us turn to the imagery. 'Batter' is undecided at first; 'knocke' suggests the familiar knocking at the heart and a Gospel reference; the 'o'erthrowing' has a touch of Jacob and the angel, but in reverse; 'breake, blowe, burn' only becomes clear from the following line where 'usurpt towne' shows that siege operations have been in the poet's mind from the beginning, mingled with other images, and 'Batter' now gains its full significance: God is the ram (not here the Lamb, we should like to say, but that is a reader's comment, no implication of the poetry). 'Reason your viceroy in mee' expresses a typically elaborate Elizabethan-Jacobean analogy, in the mediaeval tradition: the threefold relationship between heaven, the human individual (man, the microcosm) and the body politic—we notice that God is the true King of man, Reason a mere viceroy. Then we go on to sex and marriage, the analogy of heavenly and earthly love so frequent in mystical writings and especially exploited in the Baroque age. Donne's use of it is restrained: 'Nor ever chast, except you ravish mee' is not, I think, in bad taste, as has sometimes been said; the paradox is so purely of the intellect that we are left marvelling at the power and self-possession which can explore such ideas without running into those nauseating half-sublimations from which Crashaw, for instance, at times suffers.

After contemplating Donne's triumphant success we are momentarily, perhaps, reconciled to
the apologists for Group A. But may there not be
different kinds of poetic success, different poetic
aims employing different means and leading to
different yet equally valid results? To my own
mind a question is being begged when we use
terms such as 'concrete' or 'immediacy' to imply a
judgement of superior value. Are words used to
their fullest capacity more truly in the Donne
sonnet than in a line of Tennyson?—

> *And on a sudden, lo! the level lake,*
> *And the long glories of the winter moon.*

There are no stresses and strains here—but they
would spoil the picture; instead we have the alliteration in 'l' and the melodious 'moon'. The
language is formal, not colloquial, but the theme
is neither personal nor social. There is no subtlety
and no particularity, no element of contrast in the
scene. But Tennyson's picture is not of this or that
lake; it is a lake in legend, where the passing of
Arthur is mysteriously to happen. So we are told
that it is 'level': calm after storm, peace after war;
and the moonlight is presented Miltonically by its
'glories', an emotive rather than descriptive word.
'Long' is unexpected, colourless yet clearly in
place: it suggests the lowness of the moon, perhaps
also its long ascendancy in the winter sky; and the
sound of the word weaves into the peaceful pattern. By Group A standards these words are not
doing much. There is no strenuosity—but we do
not want it here; if vague emotional suggestion
and the generalized pictorial be permissible in

poetry, then the physical qualities of Tennyson's
words are adequately used. The really important
thing about the Donne sonnet, however, which
alone justifies its physical shocks and strains, is its
subtle, complex thinking—thinking carried out
in the white heat of emotion, binding together
diverse fields of experience in one strong, unified
and significant mental act. Donne's poems are not
reflections done into verse; they are truly acts of
the mind: we feel that he is analysing and orga-
nizing his experience as he writes and his last line
rounds off and signalizes a simultaneous achieve-
ment of thought. Feelings may be his subject-
matter and his thinking passionate, yet it is undoubtedly the intellect that predominates—not,
of course, the skeleton Reason of the eighteenth
century but the intellect which is the full man
energetically confronting experience. To contrast
Tennyson we need more than the two lines I have
quoted. Here is a familiar lyric:

> *Tears, idle tears, I know not what they mean,*
> *Tears from the depth of some divine despair*
> *Rise in the heart, and gather to the eyes,*
> *In looking on the happy Autumn fields,*
> *And thinking of the days that are no more.*
>
> *Fresh as the first beam glittering on a sail,*
> *That brings our friends up from the underworld,*
> *Sad as the last which reddens over one*
> *That sinks with all we love below the verge;*
> *So sad, so fresh, the days that are no more.*
>
> *Ah, sad and strange as in dark summer dawns*
> *The earliest pipe of half-awaken'd birds*
> *To dying ears, when unto dying eyes*
> *The casement slowly grows a glimmering square;*
> *So sad, so strange, the days that are no more.*

71

Dear as remember'd kisses after death,
And sweet as those by hopeless fancy feign'd
On lips that are for others; deep as love,
Deep as first love, and wild with all regret;
O Death in Life, the days that are no more.

Dr Leavis dealt rather hardly with this poem in an article in *Scrutiny* about a year ago (Vol. XIII, No. 1; Spring, 1945). Admitting 'its author's highly personal distinction', he objects to the 'sweetly plangent flow, without check, cross-tension or any qualifying element'. 'The particularity of "the happy Autumn fields", "the first beam glittering on a sail", and the casement that "slowly fades (*sic*) a glimmering square", and so on' is not the sort of particularity he requires, since 'no new definitions or directions of feeling derive from these suggestions of imagery, which seem to be wholly *of* the current of vague emotion that determines them'. It seems to me significant of Dr Leavis's limitations as a critic that he comes no closer than this to Tennyson's poem, although it is in detailed analysis that he particularly excels. Perhaps he would reply that the limitations are in the poem, and it is true that the critic has less to be busy upon in this sort of poetry—which does not in itself mean that the poetry is inferior. In contrast with Tennyson's lyric Dr Leavis presents D. H. Lawrence's *Piano,* which Dr Richards uses in his *Practical Criticism*: 'Softly, in the dusk, a woman is singing to me'. It is a poem of childhood memories and tears, which I have always thought to be vulgar, clumsy, unlovely and a mess of clichés. Dr Leavis prefers it to the Tennyson principally because Lawrence tries to resist the temptation to

weep over the past, and also because his memories
are not romantic but 'unbeglamouring' ('hymns
in the cosy parlour, the tinkling piano our guide').
I do not myself think that the presence of phrases
like 'In spite of myself' and 'my manhood is cast/
Down in the flood of remembrance' does much to
alleviate the heavy emotionality of the piece, and
though there is certainly little glamour about the
remembered hymns, they *are* treated sentiment-
ally—Lawrence does not remember what a hymn
is. But Dr Leavis sees, in Lawrence's resistance to
the past and the tension that this sets up, an emotional complexity which transvaluates the clichés
(if the complexity were really pervasive, it should
have reformed them altogether); the poem, we are
told, has the quality of 'poise'—a favourite word
with the writers in *Scrutiny*—and it is even significant that the feet of the woman at the piano are
'poised'. But the most remarkable thing about Dr
Leavis's treatment of these two poems is that here
the 'internal judgement', which distinguished
Group A from Group B and approved the former,
becomes externalized. The Tennyson is frowned
upon, not for any lack of 'immediacy' or other
such qualities—'it exhibits its author's highly
personal distinction'—but strictly 'on grounds of
emotional and spiritual hygiene': 'habitual indulgence' of this kind 'would be . . . something to
deplore', since, though 'there is nothing gross
about the poem, . . . it unquestionably offers emotion directly, emotion for its own sake without a
justifying situation, and, in the comparison, its
inferiority to Lawrence's poem compels a largely

disparaging commentary'. Here are external standards indeed! The Tennyson is condemned out of
hand, in spite of its poetic qualities, because too
much of that sort of thing would be bad—condemnation almost as severe as that of Tennyson's
own Princess, to whom in its original context the
song is sung—a fact not referred to by Dr Leavis:

> Well needs it we should cram our ears with wool
> And so pace by,

she says, Tennyson himself not being without his
ambiguous moments. The Lawrence, on the other
hand, seems to me to be approved almost equally
on 'external' grounds, because of certain phrases
which suggest a superior moral attitude, as if this
in itself neutralized the much more frequent vul-
garity of the piece. When I speak of criticism
founded in theology I do not mean anything so
clinically remedial as this. What I mean is that the
words of a poem everywhere locally betray the
quality of the poet's insight and that that insight
will of *necessity* (there is no 'ought' about it) be
measured by our own, so that if we are Christians
our criticism will be Christian, if Marxists, Marxist,
and so on—I plead merely for the recognition of
facts and the added strength which comes of self-
knowledge. But enough of this. I do not want to
seem, either, to be accusing Dr Leavis of incon-
sistency. So far as I know he has always maintained
that criticism is ultimately moral. But he *has* maintained in addition certain other standards as to the
use of language and so forth in distinguishing
Group A from Group B, so that I welcome his
treatment of *Tears, idle tears* because it shows us

74

the final objection to the poetry of Group B: it is bad for the mind.

If we examine the Tennyson lyric more closely, remembering Donne's sonnet for contrast, we may be able to see better what Tennyson is about. Clearly it is an accomplished poem, well thought out in poetic craftsmanship: its smooth rhythm is delicately varied by shifted or lightened stresses and all the play with vowels and consonants that Tennyson so well understands and sometimes, though not here, overdoes. Repeated words in pattern provide a species of restraint ('Tears'— 'tears', 'Fresh'—'sad', 'sad'—'strange', 'dying ears' —'dying eyes', etc.); there is no 'gush', no unwary release of emotion. Yet most of the thinking undoubtedly has gone into the craftsmanship; the stuff of the poem is feeling, not thought—deliberately vague and allusive, in contrast with the sharp definition of the images that stand out clearly from the emotional haze. The design of the poet is obviously to communicate feeling—of a gentle, passive quality—scarcely to define it or stimulate thought about it. Of the tears we are frankly told 'I know not what they mean'. 'Some divine despair' is again vague, but interesting—the figure is oxymoron, since there is no despair for divinity. Yet it is the 'divine' element in human nature which allows us to indulge in retrospection and be capable of despair. We know how Donne would have pressed a point like that. With Tennyson it is scarcely realized, but it is there for us if we will take it. The images are representative, dealing with what Dr Tillyard calls 'the great common-

places': the seasons, the sea, friendship, love and
death. They are, however, individual enough in
presentation: 'the first beam glittering on a sail',
'dark summer dawns', 'half-awaken'd birds', the
'glimmering square'. And there is plenty of contrast throughout the poem, the whole mood of
which is built upon a contrast: 'divine despair', the
fullness of autumnal fruition and the ineluctible
fact that the past is past—that is the theme, 'Death
in Life' and the triumph of Time, a theme not unworthy of our occasional contemplation. But the
method is everywhere Group B: emotional suggestion building up an organized sentiment, not the
critical-passionate discrimination of Group A.

Dr Leavis himself forces the question: Is this sort
of thing justified? We might agree right away that
'habitual indulgence' in the mood of this lyric would
be a bad thing. But we all have these feelings and
it is good to have them occasionally objectified and
thus far clarified for us—good, indeed, at times to
have them aroused, if we are sinking under a purely
intellectual or mundane routine. In any event,
so far as mood is concerned, Tennyson himself
'places' the poem—quite literally—by placing it
in the context of the Princess's disapproval. But
surely our value-judgement does not end here,
with an assessment of mood! It is disturbing to find
Dr Leavis taking a psychological short cut to what
should be a critical conclusion. For, of course, a
poem is much more than the mood it expresses and
it may be appreciated without our complete acqui-
escence in the mood. What is it that gives real value
to the poem? Partly, I think, 'its author's highly per-

sonal distinction', to which Dr Leavis refers: there is positive value in its delicate craftsmanship and refined sensibility, so different from the crudities of Lawrence. If it works by emotional suggestion rather than intellectual organization, there is force of *mind* in it just the same—it is the very reverse of the mindless contemporary surrealistic riot. It is simply that the mind works differently from the Group A minds, more externally yet at a 'lower' level of consciousness: emotions are not intellectually examined but are ordered and controlled by aesthetic discrimination. Then there is the value of the sentiments, an uncynical appreciation of natural beauty and human friendship and love in the very regret which is felt at their transience. There is enough here to suggest that Dr Leavis and the Princess were both a little hasty in their judgement.

In this poem, then, we have a different way of using words from the method of Group A, a method, as we have said, of emotional suggestion rather than intellectual organization, though equally a function of the poetic mind. It would seem that the very method is morally suspect to the supporters of Group A, or Dr Leavis would hardly have been betrayed (as it seems) into abandonment of the critical discipline; if there is no strenuous intellection in the matter of the poem, they fear that they are surrendering themselves to an unworthy indulgence. Nevertheless, the Group B method has its own sanative function: it plays upon the deep and general emotions, the normal sentiments, the 'great commonplaces', feeding

77

those deep springs of the soul which can be choked
almost as readily by the constantly active intellect
as by the cares of the world. See the method at
work, for instance, in *The Passing of Arthur*, where
the misty scene and the misty half-allegory dissolve
into one another with a sense of beauty and power
and religious awe. In the border-country of the
mind more can be done by hinted emotions and the
vague pictorial than by the Group A sort of activity. There is a poetry of active thought, critical,
alert and tense, and there is a poetry of incantation.
They correspond to different but equally valid
attitudes to experience, the upreared questioning
of *homo sapiens* and the contemplative wonder of
the child of God. While we remember that both
are the same creature, that the childhood and the
rational manliness are both God's gifts, we shall
feel the need of both types of poetry that I have
attempted to examine.

IV—THE CRITICAL SITUATION

I have not yet done with Group A and Group
B, the Shakespeare-Donne type of poetry and the
Spenser-Milton-Tennyson type. We have still to consider why Group A should be especially in favour in
our time—or perhaps I should say in the generation
which is now middle-aged. The main reason is fairly
obvious: it is—or was—a sceptical age, and scepticism, especially scepticism about the capacity of the

reason, inevitably produces subtle intellection to justify its departure from common sense. The decay of dogmatic and moral certainties, of assured sentiments, left a ferment where startling novelties of thought bubbled to the surface. There was, for instance 'the new psychology'. The nineteen-twenties turned to the Jacobeans in the erroneous belief that the intellectual ferment of that period was similar to their own. It is instructive to observe how thoroughly Donne has been misunderstood through the reading into his works of a type of scepticism which he certainly never aspired to. For a time the *Songs and Sonets* were all the rage —because they were cynical about sex! In fact, as is plain from his serious writing, much of it included in the *Songs and Sonets,* Donne was remarkably secure on the subject of Christian marriage and shares with Shakespeare and the Book of Common Prayer the honour of having cleared away a great deal of highfalutin 'Platonic' rubbish and perverted piety which held in contempt the function of the body in love. Because he was so secure, he could also dash off little *jeux d'esprit* in praise of inconstancy, which are just about as far from the sober improprieties of the nineteen-twenties as anything could be. Then he was regarded as a sceptic in religion, because he said that the new philosophy calls all in doubt—no one outside academic circles bothering to find out that 'philosophy' here meant 'science' (as in the Scottish chairs of Natural Philosophy) and that he was merely commenting on the contemporary Copernican muddle. Donne was quite clear, however,

79

(see the *Second Anniversarie*) that we shall know
fully in heaven all that remains mysterious on
earth. As Sir Herbert Grierson said years ago: 'It
was not of religion he doubted but of science'.

There is, nevertheless, some analogy between the
age of Donne and the nineteen-twenties, especially
in their consciousness of the complexity of experience and their determination to cope with it, and
it is natural that more serious minds than those
we have been considering should also turn to the
early seventeenth century with particular interest.
The conventions of Georgian poetry no longer
satisfied the new situation, and the colloquial diction and wide range of imagery in the Jacobeans,
their discarding of the stock poetic tradition and
employment of the everyday or the erudite image
rather than the obviously beautiful, was bound to
be attractive. It is the weakness of the academic
not to know the history of his own times and I may
perhaps be allowed to plead that I am now outside
my period—but I imagine it was Mr Eliot's *Sacred
Wood* that really started the whole affair. His admirable analyses of the verse of certain Elizabethan
and Jacobean dramatists began the movement for
'close verbal criticism' to which we are all so much
indebted, but coupled with his early disparage-
ment of Milton (for which he has since made
amends to my mind more than sufficient) began
also the advocacy of Group A methods which his
own poetic practice had already done much to
commend. (In an aside we may note how much of
Group B has since crept into his poetry—indeed it
was never wholly absent.) The influence of Mr

TWO STREAMS FROM HELICON

Eliot on Dr Leavis has been acknowledged to be considerable. Also we had Dr I. A. Richards, whose *Principles of Literary Criticism* was a textbook for us all. The first edition came out in 1924, but it could be dated closely enough on internal evidence:

'The basis of morality, as Shelley insisted, is laid not by preachers but by poets.'

'The view that what we need in this tempestuous turmoil of change is a Rock to shelter under or to cling to, rather than an efficient aeroplane in which to ride it, is comprehensible but mistaken.'

[Of the *Divina Commedia*] 'It is true that for adequately equipped readers who can imaginatively reproduce the world outlook of Aquinas, and certain attitudes to woman and chastity, which are even more inaccessible, there is no obsolescence.'

Statements like these have now a certain old-world charm, but they and the somewhat crude psychology of the book at first partially obscured, for me at least, the quite remarkable contribution that the author was making towards the advance of literary criticism. To Dr Richards, and in particular to his *Practical Criticism,* we owe the systematizing of critical technique. But his theories tended perhaps to the undue exaltation of Group A in other minds, though not, I think, in his own. He set special value on what he called 'a systematized complex response' and, although it is clear from the context that he did not limit these responses to the active intellect, the reader might well have derived from such passages a bias in favour of the Shakespeare-Donne type of organization—a bias probably strengthened by Dr Richards's pioneer treatment of 'tone' and even more by his discus-

81

sion of the 'stock response'. This set up in the young a morbid fear of ever responding to a situation in the normal way and helped to establish the vogue of the Metaphysical poets for their esoteric qualities rather than their essential normality.

There were, of course, better reasons for renewed interest in the Metaphysicals: in an essay on Marvell, written for the tercentenary, Mr Eliot spoke of their 'alliance of levity and seriousness (by which the seriousness is intensified)', of the wit which 'involves, probably, a recognition, implicit in the expression of every experience, of other kinds of experience which are possible', and of their 'tough reasonableness beneath the slight lyric grace'. The best literary values of the period, expressed by Mr Eliot and Dr Leavis, crystallized in admiration of this highly civilized 'awareness'. A metaphysical and social 'technique' for dealing with complexity was just what the age lacked and historically the emphasis was justified. I do not think, however, that any one ever proved the inherent superiority of this quality of 'poise' over that simplicity which sees only one side of a question and pursues it with loyalty and love. No doubt both types of mind are necessary. However admirable Marvell may be at his best—and he is very fine indeed—it is significant that when he really did give himself to a cause he could write little better than doggerel about it: a civilized balance can be very crippling. The greatest poetry has no time for self-conscious defensive measures; like the highest religious experience, it can come only when the defences are down. In the essay to which

I have referred, Mr Eliot contrasted the emotional suggestion of Marvell, gathered about a core of precise reference, with the vague emotionality of nineteenth-century 'dream' poetry as exemplified in some verses of William Morris. There are good reasons for agreeing with him in preferring the former. But the reader must be prepared to catch these emotional suggestions in a few words and to fuse them with something probably very different in the next line; he must be emotionally well equipped before approaching a poem of Marvell. If the nineteen-twenties, witnessing the collapse of civilization, needed to turn to the unusually civilized seventeenth century, it may well be that we today stand in need of more drastic medicine. The danger now is the collapse of man, his divorce from nature and the obscuring of his metaphysical status. The poetry of dream, however varied, has but one real subject, the loss of glory and its restoration; in it the wanderer from Paradise laments his plight and half forgets it in a Paradise of the mind. Nature, too, is glorified—in Arcadia, in the symbolic mediaeval garden, or the half-visionary observation of nineteenth-century poets. Perhaps 'the vision and the dream' is most necessary to us today; we must begin culturally with pre-civilization as we must begin socially with the pre-political. Contemporary poetry presents a confused spectacle of rapid change (though there is a good deal of *la même chose* about it all) and there have been recent promises—or threats—of a Romantic Revival. The specimens I have seen are not impressive; they are mindlessly biological, still playing with roots and bones in the accustomed manner, or else they are parasitic—verbal echoes of the poetry of last century assembled together without coherent thought. This will not do. Group B were romantically inclined but they *organized* emotion; they did not offer a mere jumble of spare parts from a machine no longer understood. The verbal echo may arouse emotions already there, but we need meaning, in the everyday sense of the word— we need story, in fact, to rehabilitate emotions dissipated and decayed. The revival I await is one which will go back into line with tradition again, a poetry which will speak to the whole mind, whether organized about an intellectual or an emotional nucleus, whether Group A or Group B —or a compound of the two. For a poetry which regards consciousness as a misleading accident, though no doubt in tune with the age, can point nowhere except to the wilderness or the grave.

The reader will perhaps agree that, while a special devotion to the Group A type of poetry was for the nineteen-twenties historically inevitable, there is nothing in the origins of that devotion to justify us in still holding a one-sided view of our national literature. There is undoubtedly a special attraction about Group A for the critic who uses the method of close verbal analysis. After some years of lecturing I know how enjoyable it is to produce critical rabbits from poetic hats, and the Group A complexity provides more opportunities for that sort of thing—though not really so many as one might think. How often in the writings of Dr Leavis (and perhaps in one's own lectures)

the same stock examples recur! Normal Group A
is not so complex as the specimens usually cited.
Donne is not often 'on a huge hill' and even Shake-
spearean complexity, which is abundant, occurs
mainly in the later plays. The appreciation of
Group B at its true worth may require of the critic
a self-denying ordinance. His aid as an interpreter
may not be quite so necessary here, though I
incline to think that, if we once recognize the
validity of Group B methods, there will be a great
field to reclaim from the casual tillage of idle
appreciators. And justice compels us to admit that
there are more ways than one of writing good
poetry. Colloquial and 'poetic' language both have
their uses; rhythms may twist and contort along
with the sense or they may produce a more general,
incantatory effect (as in song-writing the music
may interpret the words closely and dramatically or
may proceed more formally to suggest the general
meaning); there is one organization where intellect and another where emotion is dominant. Some
legitimate types of poetry we have scarcely considered: narrative, serious and comic; 'familiar
epistles', where the style is nearly allied to prose.
With them the narrative procedure applies: the
words are secondary and should not draw attention
to themselves, since the reader's mind operates on
a 'higher' level. This would apply, with modifications, to Crabbe and to much of Morris. There is
a great deal to be said for Daniel's pellucid style, if
only he had used it to say something more interesting. The narrative poetry of Milton and Tennyson requires a double approach, that strictly appro-
85

priate to narrative being combined with the method of verbal criticism, since there is so much local poetic interest in their writing. Indeed I prefer to anthologize *Paradise Lost,* selecting those passages where the imagination glows in contemplating ancient mythology and mediaeval romance. After Mr C. S. Lewis's able apology I may perhaps accept the theological sections as orthodox, but I find it hard to accept them as good poetry, even allowing that there must be dullish patches in every long poem. In Dante theology is of the essence of the poetry but in *Paradise Lost* it seems to be an unpleasant necessity of the theme. And I like to avoid the more extreme perversions of the English language into which Milton can run at times with what one cannot help regarding as characteristic wilfulness. Spenser and Tennyson are more uniform and work more successfully up to and down from their particularly 'poetic' moments. The fact is that every poet—indeed, every poem—is unique and requires the careful and individual approach of all truly personal relationships. There are traditions and periods and schools—poets are largely made by their environment, no doubt—but all these abstractions, including Group A and Group B, fall short of describing any individual writer or particular work. It is my hope that criticism founded in theology may have helped to reveal the unrealities of that Great Schism between the two main bodies of English poetry. If our criterion is firmly taken back to the quality of poetic insight, there is no room for minor orthodoxies in the use of words. A *successful* use, of course, must be insisted on—but we remember that, facility with words or a verbal habit of mind once granted, 'successful expression' and 'insight' are the same thing. From his treatment of *Tears, idle tears* it would seem that, if pressed, Dr Leavis might go beyond relatively technical considerations and claim a superiority of moral function for Group A methods. I hope I have been able to show reason for accepting Group B on moral grounds, but I am not content to assess poetry on its ethical qualities or powers of psychic healing. Poetry is not a religion or a substitute for religion, which is what in various ways Shelley, Arnold and Dr Richards have inclined to make it and which certain hieratic attitudes in Dr Leavis might occasionally suggest. But poetry, like philosophy and theology and a good many other things, is a way to the truth; it attempts in its own mode to make statements about reality. It is not merely psychological in effect; it is metaphysical in implication. It is less than religion but more than mental sanitation. The validity of poetic statement is a matter of increasing interest to philosophers. Meanwhile we have only insight to check insight and, as prophylactic against pride, it is good to remember that the insight which organizes experience in precise collocations of words is in truth only one form of insight among many. The farmer's, the builder's, the housewife's task, as well as the poet's, can be a way to the truth in God. The poet, after all, is called a 'creator' only by courtesy; he sings for the same cause that the bird sings, because he is made that way. Wisdom is justified of all her children.

87

VIII *The English Tradition*

AFTER SAYING AT SOME length what the English tradition is not, I might fairly be expected to hazard an attempt at saying what it is. Technical distinctions in the use of language, imagery and so forth are no help here; we have already seen that the colloquial and the bardic types of poetry (Group A and Group B) can both claim to be genuinely English. If there be anything peculiarly national in our literature, it must be something more recondite, a quality shared by both these types of poetry and by our literary prose. We are involved, it seems, since our literature is an expression and a part of our national culture, in the familiar but highly controversial search for the English 'temper'. It is only in a logical sense that the 'temper' may be said to precede the literature, for literature constantly reacts back upon the nation's mood and plays an active part in determining the national tradition; it is not merely the expression of a tradition independently achieved. Indeed, in one way the English language itself, as used by our writers, seems to have originated or at least confirmed a national characteristic. Our language is unusually blessed in having two easily distinguishable ingredients, the Anglo-Saxon residuum of homely terms and the Romance element borrowed at various times from Latin Europe. Norman French we pretty thoroughly absorbed, but the direct borrowings from Latin at the Renaissance have always retained for us a distinct flavour and, according to use, may be scholarly, romantic or—quite frequently—comic (the use of 'big' words, especially when wrongly understood, is a favourite form of English humour). This contrast of Latinity with homespun phraseology is part of the English writer's stock-in-trade; there is nothing similar in Greek, Latin, French, Italian or German, and in Spanish the Arabic element was absorbed much earlier, though it probably contributes something to the colour and variety of the language. Macbeth, staring at the blood on his hands, exclaims:

> *Will all great Neptune's ocean wash this blood*
> *Clean from my hand? No; this my hand will rather*
> *The multitudinous seas incarnadine,*
> *Making the green one red—*

and the effect of the passage is gained largely through the contrast between the last two lines. It may be through this happy accident of linguistic history that our national literature seems to us to remain—and does in fact remain—'true to the kindred points of Heaven and Home'. For this surely is a national characteristic, the ability to combine exalted imagination with a firm grasp of simple and local realities.

Some of the best qualities in our literary tradition have been more than suspect of late, owing to the unholy alliance between literary criticism and a very dubious psychology. I have previously com-

mented on the attempt to make of criticism an independent science and have maintained on the contrary that the critic cannot pass a judgement of
value without reference to external standards. But
an appearance of self-contained stability may be
achieved by appropriating psychological theories
and treating them not as relative to certain preconceptions and therefore questionable but as objective matters of fact. Fact, of course, is any one's
property; an appeal to well-known facts does not
derogate from the dignity of a self-subsistent subject, and so our critics may still proclaim their
independence of standards derived from external
and controversial fields, like philosophy and theology, while carrying a great load of unexamined
assumptions misleadingly labelled as items of common knowledge. There is, for example, the use of
'escapism' or 'escapist' as a term of opprobrium.
Mr Charles Morgan, writing in the *Sunday Times*
(where, in spite of his opening announcement discussed earlier in this series, he has been doing some
good work as a 'theological' critic), says that 'the
foolish word [escapism] is dead'; but I can point
him to an article in the current *Scrutiny* (Vol.
XIII, No 3) in which 'the escapist novels of Scott'
gain a passing mention. Admittedly the writer is a
musician but he is concerned with the relation
between music and literature and is presumably
regarded as having some knowledge of the latter
subject. Why, then, is 'escape' necessarily bad?
Before deciding for or against any particular work
of 'escape' I should myself incline to take a hint
from Dr F. R. Tennant's treatment of the term

'value' in relation to persons and ends, and ask: 'Escape of whom, from what, into what?' As to the Scott enthusiast, we should reply: 'Escape of an unfortunate modern from the meaningless muddle of contemporary society into a world simpler and more beautiful, where the mind is recreated by an interesting story, in which right and wrong are clearly distinguished by Christian standards, while respect for historical tradition and the organic community is quietly inculcated'. An escapologist of this type need not fear banishment from his honourable place in the English literary tradition. The romantic novel, presenting a nobler and better way of life than our own, may well be more valuable than the realistic novel which draws attention to the cesspool at our feet. No doubt both have their functions, but the realistic novel is better suited to an age more complacent than the present. Escape to a luxury-hotel atmosphere is less desirable, but even the popular novel of that kind provides a necessary anodyne for many chronic sufferers from our social system. And to them, let us remember, the luxury hotel is a fairy palace; it will do them little harm. If the fairy tale has gone bad on us in this way, the literary critic can only point to the fact and hand over to the sociologist; it is no part of his duty to sneer at the shop-girl's dream. Instead he can clear his mind of cant by abandoning such ambiguous words as 'escapist'.

Another term much subject to abuse is 'adult' or 'mature', which is employed positively, as if there were general agreement as to what constitutes a full-grown man. I find an article in which 'Mar-

lowe's adult detachment' in the *Hero and Leander*
poem is commented on; the poet's 'own assent to
the irresistibility of love' is combined with a
'faintly amused' and even burlesque treatment at
times, and this is taken as evidence of 'maturity'.
May it not equally well be taken as a sign of im-
maturity, the eagerness of youth to prove to itself
and the world that it 'isn't taken in'? To my mind
it takes a middle-aged writer to treat well of young
love, not because he will produce this sort of 'poise'
but because he no longer stands in need of it: the
profound seriousness of Shakespeare's Florizel and
Perdita makes even Rosalind a little silly. The
'mature' Shakespeare can see the simple beauty of
these young people in love and is not ashamed to
declare it. It has often been stated that the English
novel is immature beside the novel of Russia or
France. This is a serious matter, for we can hardly
talk of the English tradition without giving great
weight to the work of Dickens. Dickens is sentimental. Perhaps Dostoievsky is not; perhaps Flau-
bert is not. I cannot be certain of what is sentimental in a nineteenth-century Russian context
and I have never yet brought myself to read Flau
bert. Dickens will gush over his hearty, generou:
old men and good and pretty young girls, especi
ally when the latter are on their death-beds; h
expresses an extreme horror of prostitution and ha
all the Victorian delicacy in treating sexual rela
tionships. By what standard are these attitudes im
mature? Too frequently maturity is measured b
cynicism about human nature and scepticism i
religion. If real maturity recognizes evil in th

world but, knowing the priority of good, remains undismayed—and this at least is the Christian attitude—I cannot see that Dickens, any more than Scott, need be in danger of rejection.

I hope we have gained courage to ignore the bogies of 'escapism' and 'maturity', for, as I see it, that other word 'sentiment', so unpopular among highbrows and abused by lowbrows in these days, is just what we need to describe the essence of the English tradition. We must distinguish it from 'sentimentality', which is misdirected or exaggerated feeling. Properly a sentiment is a system of feelings directed towards a real or ideal object; it implies a system of belief, which may quite possibly be unconsciously held ('dogmas', in Dr Demant's sense). Classical French literature is a matter of the intellect and the passions, at once cold and hot, but English literature is an affair of the heart, where passion and intellect have compounded to form fixed sentiments towards familiar objects: love and marriage, the home and children, the neighbourhood, the nation, the English Church. Literature of this sort has a superior subtlety, since criticism is always blent with sympathy: from Shallow's orchard to the Christmas festivities at Dingley Dell runs a tale of beloved folly, always with a core of sense.

Fundamentally, then, the English tradition is a tradition of sentiment—and it is on the stability of sentiments that civilizations are founded. Moreover, it is, in the broadest sense of the word, a romantic tradition; the English tendency is to 'heighten' the theme, so that the familiar landscape of Tintern, for instance, with its 'plots of cottage-ground' and sportive hedgerows, seems to glow in a religious light. Corresponding to this heightening of the familiar is the exploration of the unfamiliar; ourselves inhabitants of *Ultima Thule,* we have persistently delighted in the geographically remote or the trans-geography of fairyland and Ruritania, and remoteness in time has exerted a similar fascination. In this, as in every respect, Shakespeare is our leader. True all his life to the familiar Warwickshire scene (his local characters turn up in unlikely places: Bottom in a wood near Athens, Dogberry in Messina), he nevertheless projects a romantic world to which even the picturesque cartography of the Elizabethans would prove no guide: 'This is Illyria, lady'. We have the lion-infested Forest of Arden, tenanted by Arcadian shepherds, Warwickshire rustics, and gentlemen exiled from a Renaissance court; we have Bohemia with its unusual sea-coast and Prospero's Mediterranean-West Indian fairy isle. Again, there is the Roman world of Caesar and Antony and the ancient Britain of Lear and Cymbeline. Milton's conjuring with unfamiliar place-names is well known: those knights who in distant times

> *Jousted in Aspramont, or Montalban*
> *Damasco, or Marocco, or Trebisond,*
> *Or whom Biserta sent from Afric shore*
> *When Charlemain with all his peerage fell*
> *By Fontarabbia.*

Passing the wondrous voyage of Coleridge's Ancient Mariner, we come to Tennyson, the last great poet to be a 'best-seller', who filled the Victorian age with the romance of history and legend: that old war fought

> *Far on the ringing plains of windy Troy,*

and that other in

> *. . . the sunset bound of Lyonnesse—*
> *A land of old upheaven from the abyss*
> *By fire, to sink into the abyss again;*
> *Where fragments of forgotten peoples dwelt . . .*

This romantic note, the wonder and the mystery, with its sense of dim tracts of time and distant places, is not without religious significance, presenting a manifold universe that challenges the self-sufficiency of man and an intangible beauty that contrasts strongly with his day-to-day routine.

Yet this romantic temper is allied, as we have seen, to the feeling for home. Locality is more a mark of English literature than of the Continental literatures derived from cosmopolitan classicism. Perhaps Spain, whose native tradition sturdily resisted the imposition of a Roman civilization, is most akin to England in this respect. Both nations had long periods of flourishing local government, Spain in the Middle Ages, England at the same time and in the sixteenth and seventeenth centuries (Tudor centralization was nothing comparable to our modern bureaucracy); Shakespeare and Cervantes have the same tolerant and sympathetic treatment of the lower orders and provincial types. For the English tradition is rural rather than urban, and it is aristocratic. Shakespeare spent his working years in London but there are few images from urban life in his poetry; he must have lived mentally in Stratford all the time. The countryside with its hospitable great houses, its semi-feudal stratification and its subsistence economy—that is what Shakespeare presents as his ideal. Adam in *As You Like It*—a part traditionally assigned to Shakespeare himself—represents

> *The constant service of the antique world,*
> *When service sweat for duty, not for meed.*

Serving one family in life-long fidelity, he is prepared to give his life-savings to his young master and, though over eighty years old, follows him painfully into exile. On the other hand Corin the shepherd, in the same play, complains of his employer, who

> *. . . little recks to find the way to heaven*
> *By doing deeds of hospitality.*

Obviously his master is one of the 'new men', a commercial magnate settled on the land and turning to the industry of large-scale sheep-breeding for the overseas woollen market. Corin had once owned his own flock—in a small way, no doubt—but now he 'does not shear the fleeces that he grazes'; he has become a hired hand, one of the new tribe of farm labourers. Others do not see the rural scene with quite that combination of piety and practical wisdom to be found in Shakespeare, but the whole line of English writers displays our English devotion to the (somewhat idealized) traditional rural economy, with its local squire and J.P., its village parson, its village schoolmaster, and the yeoman farmer, who was the backbone of England before the remarkable surgery of the Great Rebellion put the London merchant in his place.

The list of names would stretch on to the crack of doom, but some we must mention: Drayton, whose nymphs are so primly English (Anglican, we suspect) and whose *Polyolbion,* an enormous topographical poem, describes the rural delights and the antiquities of our land; Herrick, with the 'cleanly-*Wantonnesse*' of his rustic festivities; the simple Walton, the far-from-simple Marvell, even Milton in his *L'Allegro.* Donne is exceptional, though an occasional phrase shows that he could appreciate the country scene, which in Herbert and Vaughan is turned to God's praise. There is rural economy in Dryden—he seems to enjoy the plain but plentiful fare described in his translated fragment, *Baucis and Philemon*—and Pope, brought up in Windsor Forest, is familiar with the pheasant's 'scarlet-circled eyes'. More important, he can protest against the transformation of good farmland into useless and vulgarly ostentatious pleasure-grounds such as Timon's villa, and look forward to the day when 'laughing Ceres' will 're-assume the land'. His portrait of the Man of Ross, the perfect country squire (a real, not a fictitious person; he died in 1724), shows that the Timons had not everywhere superseded the benevolent régime of an older and simpler aristocracy. On the Whig side Addison gave us Sir Roger, a lovable character and a loving portrait, but it is evident that, in the eyes of Mr Spectator, he is behind the times and that Sir Andrew Freeport is the man of the future. Throughout the eighteenth century Whig poets celebrate the new goddess, Trade, but in *The Deserted Village* Goldsmith, with

Johnson behind him, inveighs with true prophetic insight against the new ideas of prosperity ('Ill fares the land . . .'). Crabbe saw the grim side of country life and yet his satirical picture has a good deal that is pleasant about it and the *Tales of the Hall* take us back to a period when human relationships still remained more important than the cashnexus. It is unnecessary to do more than mention the Lake Poets, Tennyson, Dickens, *Cranford*, Trollope, Charlotte M. Yonge. George Eliot herself, for all her Positivism, had her heart in the old ways and leaves, in *Adam Bede* and the rest, a record of the countryside of her youth. Indeed, as the glory was passing from the earth, the Victorians became particularly tender over the English village and farmstead; we always grow tender and idyllic when the beloved object is passing from us.

Is the English tradition dead? The 'back to nature' movement in contemporary poetry is in the main biological rather than sentimental—back to the jungle, part of the modern repudiation of reason. This is not everywhere true, however: we have *Little Gidding* and Mr Nicholson's *Five Rivers,* both in the English local tradition, however wide their implications and however wide the difference between them. But any large-scale *literary* return to the English tradition is bound to be artificial and unsatisfactory unless there should be a parallel reform in our way of life. A nation and its literature are born—and reborn—together. The literature of twentieth-century England has been curiously un-English, a strange abortion, all head and loins. We need heart in it again. And I do not think that this can come from our little London cliques and the mindless wonders of fashionable surrealism. The English tradition is sentimental, romantic, rural (I suppose aristocracy will have to go, at least until it emerges again in better days) and, though I have not stressed this side of it, it is deeply religious. The village church, the village parson—often comic, yet usually respected—are an integral part of the picture, in which, as has been said, common things are seen in a religious light. The Church, the countryside and the poet are natural associates. Shallow was a silly old man and no doubt unimpressive on the Bench, but he remained true to Wordsworth's kindred points in his own stupid, amusing and pathetic way: 'Certain, 'tis certain; very sure, very sure: death, as the Psalmist saith, is certain to all; all shall die.—How a good yoke of bullocks at Stamford fair?'

This book is set in 12pt Baskerville, a type designed by the calligrapher and printer to the University of Cambridge, John Baskerville (1706-1775) of Birmingham.

Baskerville is a classical type-face described as a letter embodying the most precise geometrical proportions with the greatest elegance. Its sharp precision of outline, best seen on a smooth surface paper under ideal conditions of machining, makes it the forerunner of what is now known as the series of 'moderns'.

The present design was cut by Linotype & Machinery Ltd, from whose matrices it has been cast.